I0617149

MINDSET METAMORPHOSIS

A Practical and Transformative Guide in Mastering Your Mind for Growth and Success

DK KANG

CONTENTS

INTRODUCTION

Have you ever found yourself trapped in a loop of unhelpful thoughts, questioning your decisions and capabilities? You're not alone. Many of us wrestle with mental patterns that hold us back from reaching our fullest potential. This isn't just a book; it's a gateway to breaking those chains and forging a path to a life marked by growth, fulfillment, and success.

Mindset is a powerful determinant of how we interpret and respond to the world around us. It shapes our reactions to success and failure, influences our persistence in the face of challenges, and ultimately can dictate the trajectory of our lives. Transforming your mindset, therefore, isn't just about shifting how you think; it's about reshaping your entire life experience.

For many years, I faced profound personal challenges and crises. I was overwhelmed, discouraged, doubting my abilities, and utterly stuck. During this low point, I realized the immense power of mindset. A simple yet profound shift in my thought patterns began to dissolve the barriers I had built around myself. This pivotal moment underscored a critical truth: our most extraordinary limits are often those we impose on ourselves.

My wife has contributed to writing this book, and the following are her words:

> "Sixteen years of marriage has brought about some of the most joyful moments in our lifetimes and some of the most challenging circumstances we've faced. We have faced much adversity in health, marriage, finances, and transitions, and we consider ourselves to score quite high on the "adversity quotient" (AQ). The Adversity Quotient is defined as "a score that measures the ability of a person to deal with adversities in life; commonly known as the *science of resilience*" (Wikipedia), "a score that measures a person's ability to deal with life's difficulties and turn them into opportunities" (Google AI). Here are some challenges we have faced so far. In 2013 and 2016, respectively, my dad and mom passed away in the Philippines. Even as they were advanced in age, navigating grief and loss long distance was a challenge for us. As soon as we got back stateside after burying my mom, my husband lost his mentor at work to a heart attack at age 50. He was a role model for him, and he was devastated when he found out about it.
> During the years 2010-2020, we went through the painful journey of infertility, eventually ending in a complicated surgery that sealed our fate about

having children biologically. On its own, this journey took its toll physically, mentally, emotionally, and financially for both of us. Infertility was difficult for my health, as the compounding cause of endometriosis loomed over the background, taking its final bow in 2020 when I eventually had to have a total hysterectomy amid the COVID-19 pandemic. I had to be hospitalized twice during the pandemic, the first one being the most unforgettable because my husband wasn't able to be with me in the hospital. He was beside himself when he dropped me off and picked me back up a week later. The second hospitalization was the surgery that ended up with complications. I was not able to work for six months.

There were still many challenges afterward, spanning a timeline of 4 years. We moved to Texas at the end of 2016, hoping for a better life and future, but we struggled with our transition. I couldn't work due to my professional license not transferring from Missouri, and my husband was the sole breadwinner for our family from 2016 to 2019. When I decided to pursue my doctorate in physical therapy, he juggled two jobs and even worked a traveling job. Amazingly, we lived in a city that required twice our income and ten times the stress. We have moved 4x in the past eight years in Texas because of our financial challenges. My husband also lost his dad to pancreatic cancer in 2023.

After graduating from my doctorate, we had a little reprieve, only to have our worlds shaken again with a breast cancer diagnosis in January of 2024. A month after my diagnosis, my husband got terminated from his job after disclosing our circumstances to his manager and asking for a more flexible work schedule to accommodate my treatments. As devastating as this all sounds, I am grateful that he was with me during my chemo treatments.

As I am writing this, I (we) am still in the middle of cancer treatments. The road ahead is long and ambiguous. No matter how much we prepare, we don't know what life will bring. Having a resilient mind is essential to EVERYTHING. A resilient mind has helped me count my blessings, look at the positive side, and have hope for the future. Having a resilient mind has helped me endure chemotherapy and its notorious side effects by feeding my brain (and body) what it needs to survive (and thrive). Having a resilient mind has allowed me to rewire my thought patterns, overcome anxiety, and direct my body processes to where they need to be. And lastly, a resilient mind acknowledges some things that I cannot control and focuses on what I can control. As a Christian, I know that God is in control, and I am not. What I CAN control though, despite circumstances, is my mindset."

– Florena Kang

I give you our life examples because we know that life can be challenging with adversity and obstacles. The principles in this book have helped us be resilient, have a growth mindset, take action, and not let our circumstances define us. The principles outlined in this book will do the same for you as they did for us.

Mindset Metamorphosis: A practical and transformative guide in mastering your mind for growth and success is crafted to guide you step-by-step through cultivating a resilient, growth-oriented mindset. This book is structured to build logically and effectively, ensuring that each chapter informs and empowers you to make fundamental changes.

This book is for anyone who feels stuck, whether in their personal life, career, or pursuit of their passions. It's for those tired of the status quo and ready to dive deep into self-improvement. It doesn't matter where you are starting from; what matters is where you are willing to go.

In the following chapters, I share insights, research, and practical exercises designed to help you reflect on, engage with, and apply the principles discussed. You'll learn to adjust your mindset and nurture your physical well-being through fitness, meditation, sleep, nutrition, and hydration, acknowledging the indelible link between mind, body, and spirit.

What sets this book apart is its emphasis on real-world applicability and holistic approach. You'll find thought-provoking and actionable strategies for overcoming the everyday challenges of changing old habits and fostering new, empowering ones.

I invite you to engage deeply with this material. Reflect on your experiences, complete the exercises, and apply these lessons to overcome your hurdles. Remember, transforming your mindset is a profoundly personal journey, and this book guides you through each step.

Keep an open mind and heart as we embark on this journey together. Let's step forward with the courage to transform our minds and, by extension, our lives. Change is not just possible—it's within your grasp. Let this book be your guide.

Ready to transform your mindset and unlock your potential? Let's get started.

CHAPTER 1: LAYING THE FOUNDATIONS OF MINDSET TRANSFORMATION

> " *Do not conform to the pattern of this world, but be transformed by renewing your mind. Then you will be able to test and approve what God's will is—his good, pleasing and perfect will.* "
>
> — ROMANS 12:2 NIV

What if the invisible architect of your reality is something you can mold and shape? Across various fields, from psychology to business, the mindset concept has been identified as critical in determining success and personal fulfillment. This chapter is about understanding that very architect—your mindset—and learning how to master it to unlock your potential.

Your mindset is far more than just a buzzword. It is the set of beliefs that colors your interactions with the world and with yourself. It influences how you interpret setbacks, how you handle stress, and how much joy you derive from your accomplishments. Transforming your mindset, therefore, is not merely changing a single thought; it is about reshaping how you view everything from minor day-to-day events to your overarching life goals.

1.1 UNDERSTANDING MINDSET: THE KEY TO UNLOCKING POTENTIAL

 "The mind is everything. What you think you become."

— BUDDHA

Define Mindset

At its core, mindset refers to beliefs and attitudes about the world and oneself. It is the mental lens through which you view your experiences, profoundly influencing your behavior across different situations. Whether you realize it or not, your mindset impacts every decision, from how you respond to stress to the strategies you deploy to pursue your goals.

Growth vs. Fixed Mindset

The concept of mindset has been significantly shaped by the work of psychologist Dr. Carol Dweck, who introduced the idea of fixed and growth mindsets. A **fixed mindset** assumes that our character, intelligence, and creative abilities are static givens, which we can't change meaningfully. Success affirms that inherent intelligence assesses how those givens measure up against an equally fixed standard. Striving for success and avoiding failure at all costs becomes a way of maintaining the sense of being competent or skilled.

In contrast, a **growth mindset** thrives on challenge and sees failure not as evidence of unintelligence but as a heartening springboard for growth and stretching our existing abilities. With this mindset, you believe that you can enhance your abilities through dedication and hard work. This view creates a love of learning and resilience essential for great accomplishment. Virtually all great people have had these qualities.

Mindset and Potential

How does a growth mindset affect one's perception of personal potential? It opens up a world of possibilities. If you believe your abilities can be developed, the challenges become exciting rather than threatening. So rather than thinking, oh, I'm going to reveal my weaknesses, you say, wow, here's a chance to grow. Adopting a growth mindset can lead to a significantly more fulfilling life, marked by continuous learning and resilience during challenges.

Case Studies

Let's consider the case of Michael, a professional who struggled with public speaking due to a fixed mindset that told him he was inherently not a good communicator. After being introduced to the concept of a growth mindset, Michael began to approach speaking engagements as opportunities to develop his skills rather than as threats to his self-image. Over time, with practice and persistence, he elevated his public speaking skills and started enjoying these opportunities, which had once terrified him. His career took a positive turn after successfully leading several high-stakes presentations, something he had never imagined himself capable of.

Another example is Anna, a writer who received critical feedback on her first novel. Instead of spiraling into despair, she adopted a growth mindset, viewing criticism as a valuable tool for learning. This perspective allowed her to strengthen her writing significantly, and her subsequent works sold better and were critically acclaimed.

These stories illustrate how a shift in mindset from fixed to growth can transform personal and professional experiences, turning perceived limitations into launchpads for success. As we explore this book further, you'll discover that such transformations are possible and within your reach.

1.2 THE SCIENCE OF NEUROPLASTICITY: REWIRING YOUR BRAIN FOR SUCCESS

 "You can rewire your brain to change your mind, and reprogram your mind to change your body."

— CAROL KERSHAW, EDD AND BILL
WADE, PH.D.

Imagine your brain as a dynamic, ever-changing landscape, not a static entity fixed by adulthood. This is the essence of neuroplasticity. It refers to the brain's astonishing ability to reorganize itself by forming new neural connections throughout life. This capability means that neurons (nerve cells) in the brain adjust their activities in response to new situations or changes in the environment, a process that allows for learning from and adapting to different experiences. What's revolutionary about understanding neuroplasticity is that it empowers us with the knowledge that change is not just a possibility but a constant aspect of brain function.

The implications of neuroplasticity extend into the realm of mindset. Adopting a new perspective can physically alter the brain's structure. This transformation enhances the brain's ability to adapt to new challenges and learn from experiences. For instance, when you shift from a fixed mindset that views challenges as threats to a growth mindset that sees them as opportunities to evolve, your brain strengthens the neural pathways supporting learning and adaptability. This shift doesn't just help you feel differently about challenges; it actively remodels your brain to handle them better.

Certain practices can be particularly beneficial to enhance the brain's plasticity, such as *mindfulness meditation*, to enhance the brain's plasticity. *Mindfulness meditation* is a mental practice that involves focusing your mind on the present moment while calmly acknowledging and accepting your feelings, thoughts, and bodily sensations. It is often used as a therapeutic technique to reduce stress, improve focus, and promote overall well-being. Key aspects include:

1. **Attention to Breath:** Concentrating on the breath to anchor the mind in the present.
2. **Observation without Judgment:** Noticing thoughts and feelings without labeling them as good or bad.
3. **Body Scan:** Paying attention to physical sensations throughout the body, from head to toe.

4. **Present-Moment Awareness:** cultivating a heightened awareness of the present moment rather than dwelling on the past or worrying about the future.

The practice can be done seated, walking, standing, or lying down, and sessions can range from a few minutes to several hours. *Mindfulness meditation* has been shown to promote changes in brain regions associated with memory, self-awareness, and regulation of emotions. Regularly engaging in mindfulness practices can cultivate a brain better equipped to cope with stress and more adept at remaining focused and calm in various situations. Similarly, learning new skills, whether a language, instrument or even a new sport, can stimulate neural growth and flexibility. Each time you step out of your comfort zone to learn something new, you're accumulating knowledge and physically expanding your brain's capacity.

The benefits of a brain enhanced by neuroplasticity are immense. Individuals with a high degree of neuroplasticity exhibit better problem-solving skills, an improved memory, and greater emotional resilience. They are better at making connections between disparate ideas, more creative, and more adept at navigating social situations. Consider, for instance, the case of a manager who, through dedicated practice in emotional intelligence training, expanded his leadership skills and reported less stress and greater satisfaction in his professional and personal life. This example highlights how the brain's flexibility can significantly improve all areas of life, underscoring the profound impact of cultivating a mindset that embraces growth and learning.

As we continue to explore the power of mindset and neuro-plasticity, remember that the capacity for change is wired into the very fabric of your brain. Every challenge encountered, and every new skill learned represents an opportunity for growth and serves as a catalyst for physical changes in your brain that enhance your ability to thrive in a complex world. This understanding not only liberates us from misconceptions about our limitations but also invites us to approach life with a new perspective that enthusiastically embraces change and growth.

1.3 IDENTIFYING LIMITING BELIEFS AND OVERCOMING SELF-DOUBT

 "Believe in yourself and all that you are. Know that there is something inside you that is greater than any obstacle."

— CHRISTIAN D. LARSON

Limiting beliefs are the silent saboteurs lurking in the shadows of our subconscious, often going unrecognized yet significantly impacting our behavior and mindset. These beliefs can manifest as doubts about our abilities, fears of failure or success, or more profound, more ingrained notions such as imposter syndrome—the persistent belief that one is not as competent as others perceive them to be and that one day they will be exposed as a "fraud." Understanding and addressing these beliefs is imperative for anyone looking to foster a growth-oriented mindset and achieve personal success.

The first step in overcoming these debilitating beliefs is to identify them. This might involve reflecting on areas where you feel stuck or repeatedly encounter obstacles. For instance, a common limiting belief is "I am not good enough to be successful," which can prevent individuals from pursuing higher career opportunities or personal goals. Another might be "I must not fail," which can stifle creativity and risk-taking, essential components of growth and innovation. Recognizing these beliefs is like turning on a light in a previously dark room—suddenly, the obstacles you couldn't tackle become visible, and you can begin to navigate through them.

Once these beliefs are identified, challenging and reframing them can begin. Techniques such as *journaling* can be particularly effective here. By writing down your limiting beliefs, you externalize them, making them less daunting and more manageable. This practice also allows you to reflect on the roots of these beliefs and question their validity. Cognitive-behavioral techniques are also invaluable in this process. For example, *cognitive restructuring*, a method used in cognitive-behavioral therapy, involves identifying and disputing irrational or maladaptive thoughts. You can weaken their hold over your mind by systematically challenging these limiting beliefs.

Mindfulness meditation offers another powerful tool for dealing with limiting beliefs. It allows you to observe your thoughts and feelings without judgment, providing a clearer perspective on your mental patterns. Regular mindfulness practice teaches you to detach from harmful beliefs and view them as thoughts that pass through your mind rather than truths that define your reality.

Building self-confidence and reducing self-doubt are equally crucial in this journey. Setting small, manageable goals and celebrating when you achieve them can boost your confidence and gradually dismantle the power of self-doubt. This incremental approach affirms that you can achieve your goals and builds a positive momentum that makes more considerable successes more attainable.

Personal stories of transformation underscore the power of overcoming limiting beliefs. Consider the case of Linda, a talented artist who believed she could never turn her passion into a career because she thought she wasn't gifted enough to compete professionally. This belief held her back for years until she began to question its validity. Through journaling and cognitive-behavioral techniques, Linda challenged her self-doubt, and gradually, her mindset shifted. She started to see opportunities instead of obstacles. Today, Linda runs a successful art studio and has sold her work to clients worldwide. Her story is a testament to the profound impact that reshaping your mindset can have on your life's path.

As we delve deeper into mindset transformation strategies, remember that personal growth is not about reaching a destination. It is about continually striving to understand yourself better, challenging the beliefs that hold you back, and equipping yourself with the tools to grow and succeed. The path may not always be easy, but the rewards of a liberated, growth-oriented mindset are immeasurable.

1.4 THE ROLE OF SELF-AWARENESS IN PERSONAL TRANSFORMATION

 "Knowing yourself is the beginning of all wisdom."

— ARISTOTLE

Self-awareness is akin to looking into a mirror, not to scrutinize your external appearance but to understand the deeper contours of your character, emotions, and desires. It involves a conscious awareness of one's internal states, a crucial aspect often overlooked in the quest for personal and professional success. This awareness is the bedrock upon which you can build a solid understanding of your current mindset, revealing how your thoughts, feelings, and behaviors are aligned—or misaligned—with your life's goals and values.

Increasing self-awareness is not merely an exercise in introspection; it's a strategic tool that can lead to more effective decision-making, improved relationships, and more significant personal and professional growth. Techniques for enhancing self-awareness are varied, but the most effective are meditation, feedback analysis, and personality tests. Meditation, particularly mindfulness meditation, encourages you to observe your thoughts and feelings without judgment, creating a space to recognize patterns without being overwhelmed. This practice can help you detach from reactive emotional patterns and clarify your intrinsic motivations.

Feedback analysis, another critical tool, involves systematically collecting and analyzing feedback on your behaviors and outcomes. This can be particularly enlightening in a professional context, where specific feedback can uncover blind spots in your leadership or communication styles. Similarly, personality tests like the Myers-Briggs Type Indicator or the Enneagram provide a structured way of understanding your personality traits, offering insights into how these traits influence your interactions and decisions.

The journey towards enhanced self-awareness is profoundly personal, yet its impact extends beyond the individual. For instance, consider the transformation of Emma, a marketing executive whose aggressive pursuit of career success was marred by frequent conflicts with colleagues. Through feedback analysis, Emma discovered that her communication style was often perceived as abrasive. This realization was unsettling but pivotal. By embracing mindfulness practices, she began to understand the roots of her aggressive behavior, tracing them back to insecurities that she hadn't acknowledged before. This newfound awareness allowed her to modify her interactions, leading to more harmonious relationships and a supportive team environment.

In another case, Robert, a school teacher, found himself disenchanted with his profession. Using personality tests, he uncovered a strong inclination towards careers that offered more autonomy and creativity than his current role allowed. This insight motivated a career shift that led to his educational consultancy, aligning his work with his inner desires and strengths. His story highlights how self-awareness can direct us toward paths that resonate more deeply with our core being, enhancing satisfaction and fulfillment in our professional lives.

Self-awareness also plays a crucial role in personal relationships. Understanding your emotional patterns, triggers, and communication styles allows you to navigate interactions more effectively, reducing misunderstandings and deepening connections. This was evident in the case of Lydia and Paul, a couple who struggled with recurring conflicts. Through joint sessions of mindfulness-based relationship counseling, they became aware of the underlying patterns in their interactions. Paul recognized his tendency to withdraw in conflict, a behavior that triggered Lydia's fear of abandonment. This awareness broke their cycle of conflict, allowing them to establish a more open and supportive way of communicating.

These narratives underscore that self-awareness is about knowing yourself and understanding how you relate to the world around you. It empowers you to make proactive changes that are not merely reactive but proactive, fostering a life more aligned with your aspirations and values. As we delve deeper into the transformative power of self-awareness, remember that each step towards understanding yourself better is a step towards a more fulfilling and authentic life.

1.5 SETTING INTENTIONS FOR GROWTH: THE FIRST STEP TOWARDS CHANGE

 "The best time to plant a tree was 20 years ago. The second-best time is now"

— CHINESE PROVERB

The subtle yet profound act of setting intentions begins a personal evolution. Intentions are not just goals or resolutions; they represent a holistic commitment to how you live every day, influencing your actions and outcomes. Unlike goals, which are often future-focused and specific, intentions are lived each day and are aligned with your core values and sense of purpose. They serve as a compass, guiding your decisions and behaviors, ensuring they reflect your deepest desires and aspirations.

The Power of Intentions

Setting powerful intentions is akin to planting seeds in a fertile garden of your mind. Just as seeds need the right conditions to grow, intentions require a nurturing environment of thought and action. When you set an intention, you declare to yourself and the universe how you choose to show up in every moment. Whether approaching your work with creativity and enthusiasm, engaging with your family with an open heart, or cultivating kindness and compassion towards yourself and others, each intention gently steers your life toward these values. The beauty of intentions lies in their ability to shape your daily experiences and interactions, making every moment an opportunity to manifest the qualities you wish to embody.

How to Set Effective Intentions

Creating intentions that resonate deeply and have the power to transform your life involves several key steps. First, reflect on what matters most to you. What are your core values? What qualities do you wish to cultivate in yourself? Answers to these questions form the foundation of effective intentions. Next, articulate these intentions with clarity and positivity. Instead of vague or negative statements, frame your intentions in precise, positive language. For instance, instead of saying, "I will stop being so negative," you might say, "I intend to embrace positivity and optimism each day." This positive framing reinforces the quality you wish to develop, making it more likely to manifest in your daily life.

It's also crucial to ensure that your intentions are actionable and measurable. While intentions are more about the journey than the destination, having a way to check your alignment with these intentions can be incredibly helpful. For example, suppose you intend to nurture your health and well-being. In that case, you might set measurable parameters like meditating for 20 minutes daily or preparing three healthy meals weekly. These measurable actions help keep your intentions grounded in everyday reality, making them more tangible and attainable.

Aligning Intentions with Values

The most powerful intentions are those aligned with your values. This alignment ensures that your intentions guide your daily choices and behaviors and resonate with your deeper self, providing a sense of purpose and satisfaction. To align your intentions with your values, start by thoroughly assessing the values most important to you. These might include creativity, compassion, integrity, or resilience; once you've identified these values, craft intentions that promote and reflect these values in your daily life. For instance, if integrity is your core value, an intention could be, "I intend to interact honestly and transparently in all my communications."

Examples of Intentions That Led to Success

Consider the story of Clara, a corporate lawyer who set the intention to lead with empathy and mindfulness. Despite her industry's high-pressure, often cutthroat environment, Clara's intention allowed her to foster a collaborative and supportive atmosphere among her team. This improved the team's productivity and morale and enhanced Clara's leadership skills, leading to her promotion to a senior partner position. Her success was a direct result of her commitment to her intention, which was carefully chosen to reflect her values of leadership and compassion.

Another example is James, a school teacher who intended to be more present and engaged with his students. By consciously setting this intention at the start of each day, James found that he was more attentive and responsive to his student's needs, significantly improving his effectiveness as a teacher. His students' performance improved markedly, and James found greater satisfaction and fulfillment in his teaching, reaffirming the power of well-aligned intentions.

These examples highlight the transformative power of setting well-defined, actionable, and deeply aligned intentions with personal values. As you move forward, consider how setting your intentions could catalyze personal and professional growth. Whether fostering better relationships, achieving career success, or enhancing personal well-being, the right intentions can set the foundation for a fulfilling and purposeful life.

1.6 BUILDING A PERSONAL VISION BOARD: VISUALIZING SUCCESS

 "Visualize this thing that you want, see it, feel it, believe in it. Make your mental blueprint, and begin to build."

— ROBERT COLLIER

Imagine a powerful tool that serves as a daily reminder of your aspirations, channeling your focus and reinforcing your commitment to your goals. This is the essence of a vision board—a tangible representation of your dreams and objectives. A vision board is more than just a collage of images; it's a curated collection that symbolizes your highest aspirations and is a constant source of motivation and inspiration.

Purpose of a Vision Board

A vision board operates on the principle of 'seeing is believing.' By visually representing your goals, you make them more accurate and attainable. Selecting images and words that resonate with your desires and displaying them where you'll see them daily helps keep your attention focused on your intentions. This practice keeps you aligned with your objectives and activates powerful psychological tools of visualization that can influence your subconscious mind, steering your actions and decisions toward your goals.

Creating a Vision Board

Creating a vision board is both an artistic endeavor and a strategic activity. Start with a clear and calm mind, perhaps after a meditation or a peaceful walk, to connect deeply with your aspirations. Gather materials such as a poster board, magazines, printouts, markers, and glue. As you sift through these materials, look for images and words that vividly represent your goals and evoke strong positive emotions. These could be pictures of places you want to travel, symbols of health like fruits or yoga poses, or words that capture feelings of success and happiness.

Place these elements on your board in a way that feels aesthetically pleasing and meaningful. Each image and word should serve as a potent reminder of your goals, covering personal, professional, spiritual, and emotional growth. Once completed, hang your vision board where you will see it daily—such as your bedroom, home office, or personal space. This visibility ensures that your goals are imagined and woven into the fabric of your daily life, constantly reminding you of the direction you wish to move towards.

The Psychology Behind Visualization

The power of visualization is well-documented in psychological research. Visualization activates the same neural networks that actual task performance does, which means that visualizing success can 'trick' the brain into thinking you've already achieved your goals, increasing your inner drive to pursue them. This mental rehearsal primes you for action, enhances motivation, and boosts confidence. Furthermore, regularly seeing your goals' visual representation helps maintain focus and prevents you from being distracted by less important tasks. This focused attention is crucial in a world brimming with distractions that can lead to procrastination or disengagement from one's goals.

Success Stories

Many attribute significant personal and professional achievements to using vision boards. For instance, a young entrepreneur named Sarah credited her vision board with helping her launch her marketing firm. She had placed images of bustling office space, happy clients, and inspiring business quotes on her board. Seeing these images daily while working from her small initial office kept her motivated, and within two years, she had grown her business to match the vision on her board.

Another compelling story comes from Mark, a freelance graphic designer who aspired to work on major film projects. His vision board was filled with logos of top film studios, mock movie posters with his name, and luxurious travel destinations for film shoots. This constant visual reminder fueled his ambition and focus, leading him to pitch to significant studios successfully, ultimately landing a project with a renowned director.

These stories underline the transformative potential of maintaining and visualizing a personal vision board. You create a powerful visual affirmation of your capabilities and goals by articulating your dreams and regularly engaging with them through your board. This process inspires you and propels you to realize your most cherished dreams.

In wrapping up, consider your vision board as a dynamic tool. As your goals evolve, so too should your board. Regularly updating it to reflect your new interests, aspirations, and objectives keeps your motivations fresh and your actions aligned with your true intentions. This continual process of reflection and revision is crucial as it ensures that your vision board remains relevant, inspiring, and closely tied to the person you are becoming. By faithfully integrating this tool into your personal development strategy, you set the stage for a life of fulfillment and achievement, visually guided by your deepest desires and aspirations.

CHAPTER CHALLENGES

1. Adopt a growth mindset: Learn something new (like a new language). Attend a seminar and take online courses on whatever you desire to learn. Continue to do this and see how much you can learn every year.
2. Be self-aware: Meditate for at least 5 minutes daily to observe your thoughts, gradually increasing to 20 minutes.
3. Be intentional: For at least 30 minutes every day, be deliberate and engaged in 1 area of your life where you give your undivided attention, whether work, family, hobby, or whatever you choose.
4. Create a vision board: Make a personal vision board of your goals or dreams and place it somewhere you can see it daily and continue to add to the vision board once a week.

CHAPTER 2: PRACTICAL STRATEGIES FOR OVERCOMING COMMON MINDSET OBSTACLES

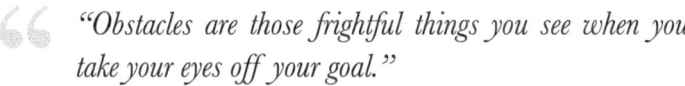 *"Obstacles are those frightful things you see when you take your eyes off your goal."*

— HENRY FORD

I magine standing at the edge of a cliff, the path forward obscured by fog. This image often mirrors our experiences with procrastination—knowing what we need to do but unable to leap due to unseen psychological barriers that keep us from moving forward. Overcoming procrastination isn't merely about better time management or stronger willpower; it's about understanding and addressing the deeper emotional and cognitive reasons behind our reluctance to act. This chapter delves into practical strategies to conquer procrastination, transforming it from a formidable foe into a manageable aspect of life. By breaking down tasks, employing time-boxing, and celebrating progress, you can create a productive rhythm that sustains your motivation and propels you towards your goals.

2.1 STRATEGIES TO BEAT PROCRASTINATION: GETTING STARTED IS HALF DONE

 "The greatest amount of wasted time is the time not getting started."

— DAWSON TROTMAN

Identify Procrastination Triggers

The first step in conquering procrastination is identifying what triggers it. These triggers can be as diverse as fear of failure, fear of success, a lack of interest, or even an unclear task. For many, the fear of failure is paralyzing—you might avoid starting a task because you're afraid the final product won't be perfect or received well. Conversely, a fear of success might subconsciously worry you because of the increased responsibilities success might bring. Understanding these triggers is crucial because it allows you to address your procrastination's root causes directly. By acknowledging and understanding your fears, you can dismantle them, clearing the path for action.

Break Tasks into Smaller Steps

One effective strategy to combat the daunting feeling of a big project is to break it into smaller, more manageable parts. This approach reduces intimidation and can help clear the mental block often accompanying large, complex tasks. Start by outlining the major components of the task, then break these components down into smaller steps that can be accomplished in one sitting. For instance, if you're tasked with writing a report, you could break it down into stages such as research, outlining, writing the first draft, revising, and final editing. Each step feels more achievable, and crossing each off your list can motivate you to the next step.

Use Time-boxing

Time-boxing is a highly effective time management technique where you allocate a fixed time to a particular task and then move on to another task once the time expires, regardless of whether the first task is completed. This method not only helps enhance focus and efficiency by creating a sense of urgency but also helps overcome perfectionism by limiting the amount of time you can spend on a task. For example, you may spend only 30 minutes on email each morning or two hours on a project proposal. Doing so ensures you make the right effort on each task, preserving your energy and attention for other essential daily activities.

Reward Progress

Setting up a reward system can be an excellent way to maintain motivation and reduce the allure of procrastination. Rewards can reinforce positive behavior and provide something to look forward to once a task or a set of tasks is completed. The key is ensuring the rewards are meaningful and frequent enough to keep your motivation high. For instance, after completing a challenging report, you might treat yourself to a favorite coffee or take a break to watch an episode of a show you enjoy. For larger projects, the rewards can be more substantial, such as a nice dinner out or a small trip. This strategy makes the process more enjoyable and forms a positive association with completing tasks.

By implementing these strategies, you can transform procrastination from a recurring issue into a manageable part of your productivity toolbox. Remember, the goal isn't to eliminate procrastination—everyone procrastinates to some extent—but to control it so that it doesn't hinder your progress and success. Each small step in overcoming procrastination builds your confidence and reinforces your ability to manage your tasks and time effectively, paving the way for increased productivity and success in all areas of your life.

Tools and techniques for Mastering time management

Effective time management is an anchor in the swirl of our daily routines, helping us navigate tasks with precision and calmness. It's not merely about squeezing as many tasks into your day as possible; it's about identifying what needs your attention and when. One of the most effective ways to bring this clarity into your life is through the Eisenhower Box—a simple yet powerful tool for task prioritization. The **Eisenhower Box**, named after Dwight D. Eisenhower, who used this method, divides tasks into four categories: urgent and important, important but not urgent, urgent but not important, and neither urgent nor important. Using this matrix, you can visualize where your activities fall and adjust your focus accordingly.

For instance, tasks that are urgent and important should be done immediately. These tasks require immediate attention and have significant consequences if delayed. On the other hand, tasks that are important but not urgent are the ones that contribute to long-term missions and goals. Scheduling specific times to handle these tasks can help advance your personal and professional growth without the pressure of an impending deadline. Tasks that are urgent but not important are often the ones that demand attention because of other people's needs. Here, delegation is critical. Lastly, tasks that are neither urgent nor important should be minimized or eliminated. They tend to be distractions that drain time and energy from your day. By sorting your tasks into these categories, you can ensure that your energy and attention are directed to the tasks that truly matter, enhancing your productivity and sense of fulfillment.

Another cornerstone of effective time management is the **Pomodoro Technique**, a time management method developed by Francesco Cirillo in the late 1980s. This technique uses a timer to break work into intervals, traditionally 25 minutes in length, separated by short breaks. Each interval is known as a "Pomodoro," named after the tomato-shaped kitchen timer Cirillo used as a university student. Here's how it works: you pick a task, set the timer for 25 minutes, and work uninterrupted until the timer rings. Then, take a short break (5 minutes), which clears your mind and rejuvenates you for the next round. After four Pomodoros, take a more extended break (15-30 minutes), which helps you recover and maintain your mental agility for longer focused work. This technique helps maintain concentration and combat fatigue, ensuring you remain consistently productive throughout the day.

Leveraging technology effectively can also transform your approach to managing time. Numerous apps and digital tools are designed to streamline task management and enhance productivity. Apps like Trello, Asana, and

Monday.com allow you to organize tasks visually and track their progress. These tools are handy for collaborative projects where multiple stakeholders need updates on the task's progress. Moreover, tools like Google Calendar or Microsoft Outlook can help with scheduling and remind you about necessary appointments and deadlines. Using these tools can free up mental space and reduce the stress of remembering every detail, allowing you to focus more on the task.

Lastly, setting clear, actionable goals must be balanced. This is where **SMART** Goals—Specific, Measurable, Achievable, Relevant, and Time-bound—come into play. By ensuring your goals meet these criteria, you can create a roadmap that specifies what you aim to achieve and outlines how to measure progress, what resources are required, why the goal is essential, and the timeframe for achieving it. For example, instead of setting a vague goal like "get more clients," a SMART goal would be "acquire three new clients for my freelance graphic design business within the next two months by networking with local businesses and promoting my services on social media." This clarity makes the goal more tangible and the path forward more understandable, significantly increasing your chances of success. The SMART goals will be further discussed in Chapter 8.

By applying these strategies, you can master the art of time management, turning what often feels like a frantic rush against the clock into a well-orchestrated symphony of productivity. Whether it's through prioritizing tasks with the Eisenhower Box, enhancing focus with the Pomodoro Technique, utilizing digital tools to streamline your schedule, or setting SMART goals, the mastery of time management is within your reach.

2.2 TRANSFORMING NEGATIVE SELF-TALK INTO A POSITIVE NARRATIVE

 "Once you replace negative thoughts with positive ones, you'll start having positive results."

— WILLIE NELSON

The words we whisper to ourselves have immense power to uplift, belittle, inspire, and discourage. Negative self-talk, a common habit among many, can be a significant obstacle to achieving one's full potential. It often operates under the radar, subtly influencing feelings and behaviors in ways that might not be immediately obvious. Recognizing these patterns is the first vital step toward reclaiming the narrative of your mind and steering it toward positivity and growth.

Negative self-talk often surfaces in moments of stress or uncertainty, whispering reminders of past failures or painting gloomy predictions. You might think, "I'm not good enough to handle this," or "I always mess this up." Such thoughts erode self-esteem and paralyze action. Awareness of these patterns is crucial because it marks the beginning of your ability to change them. Start by observing your inner dialogue, especially when anxious or stressed. Write these thoughts down—it makes them easier to confront and manage. Recognizing that these negative statements are a product of your fears, not necessarily reflections of reality, is a powerful insight that sets the stage for transformation.

Once you've identified negative self-talk patterns, the next step is *reframing* these thoughts into positive affirmations that empower and motivate. Reframing doesn't mean ignoring reality or engaging in wishful thinking; instead, it's about shifting your perspective to a more balanced and constructive viewpoint. For instance, instead of saying, "I always mess this up," you could reframe it to, "Every mistake is a learning opportunity." This doesn't dismiss the fact that mistakes happen but changes the focus from self-criticism to self-improvement. Similarly, replacing "I'm not good enough to handle this" with "I have handled challenging situations before, and I can learn from this experience, too" shifts the narrative from a fixed mindset to a growth mindset. This process of reframing is a potent tool that combats negativity and fosters a resilient and proactive attitude towards life's challenges.

In addition to reframing thoughts, practicing self-compassion is essential in mitigating negative self-talk. Self-compassion involves treating yourself with the same kindness and understanding that you would offer a good friend. It's about recognizing that perfection is impossible and all humans are works in progress. When you catch yourself slipping into self-criticism, pause and ask yourself, "Would I speak to someone I care about in this way?" If the answer is no, take a moment to soften your tone and offer encouragement and support. Cultivating self-compassion can be reinforced through mindfulness meditation, which helps you become more aware of your thoughts and feelings without judgment, allowing you to meet your experiences with kindness and understanding rather than harsh criticism.

Finally, *cognitive behavioral therapy (CBT)* techniques can be incredibly effective in changing the narrative of your internal dialogues. CBT is based on the idea that our thoughts, feelings, and behaviors are interconnected and that changing one can change the others. One basic CBT technique is the 'thought record,' which involves writing down negative thoughts, identifying the emotions and behaviors they provoke, and then challenging these thoughts by considering alternative, more balanced perspectives. For example, if you're thinking, "I'm going to fail this project," list the evidence that supports and contradicts this view. This might include past successes or instances where you've overcome similar challenges. This exercise helps recognize cognitive distortions and develop more rational, balanced thoughts.

By engaging in these practices, you actively participate in the reshaping of your mental landscape. The transformation from negative to positive self-talk is not an overnight change, nor is it always a linear process. It requires patience, persistence, and a gentle yet firm commitment to steering your inner dialogue towards empowerment and positivity. The effort to transform your self-talk is a profound investment in yourself that can radically alter your approach to life's challenges and expand your capacity for joy and achievement.

2.3 DEALING WITH OVERWHELM: STEPS TO REGAIN CONTROL

 "Do not let circumstances control you. You change your circumstances."

— JACKIE CHAN

In the fast-paced rhythm of modern life, feeling overwhelmed isn't just a rare inconvenience; it's often a persistent state for many. Whether it's due to mounting pressures at work, complex family dynamics, or the ceaseless flow of information and demands on our attention, the weight can pull your mental and physical health into a downward spiral. Recognizing when you're overwhelmed is the first crucial step to regaining control. This can manifest in various ways: you notice a tightness in your chest, a constant sense of urgency, or even forgetfulness. Emotionally, overwhelm can leave you feeling irritable, anxious, or detached. Each person might experience these symptoms differently, but the common thread is a noticeable decline in your ability to function efficiently and calmly.

Once you pinpoint these signs, integrating mindfulness and meditation into your daily routine can be transformative. These practices anchor you in the present moment, providing a break from the relentless cycle of worry and rumination accompanying overwhelm. Mindfulness involves observing your current experiences without judgment—acknowledging thoughts as they come but letting them pass without getting entangled. Meanwhile, meditation can vary from focusing on your breath, reciting a calming mantra, or engaging in guided imagery. Each technique offers a mental respite, effectively hitting the pause button on the chaos, allowing you to regain clarity and focus. Regular practice alleviates immediate stress and builds your resilience against future overwhelm.

Delegation is another vital strategy. It involves a conscious decision to pass on tasks others can handle or even handle better. This is particularly relevant in a workplace where the urge to take on every task yourself can be intense. Start by identifying tasks that do not require your specific skill set or are routine and time-consuming. Delegating these can free up a significant amount of your time and mental space, allowing you to focus on crucial tasks that play to your strengths. If you're a leader, effective delegation also empowers your team, allowing them to grow and develop new skills, which can improve overall team performance and morale.

Finally, the importance of taking *regular, scheduled breaks* must be balanced. While it might seem counterintuitive to pause when there's so much to do, taking breaks is essential to maintain long-term productivity and creativity. These breaks could be as simple as a five-minute walk, a quick stretch, or a moment to step outside for fresh air. The key is to make these breaks a non-negotiable part of your schedule. Regular disengagement from work refreshes your mind, offering new perspectives and recharging your mental batteries. For those who work in highly demanding environments, consider implementing longer breaks or quiet periods where you can disconnect completely from work-related tasks. This prevents burnout and preserves enthusiasm and engagement with work and personal life.

Adopting these strategies transforms overwhelming situations from barriers into manageable elements of your life. Each step, whether recognizing the signs of overwhelm, practicing mindfulness, delegating tasks, or committing to regular breaks, builds on the last, creating a robust framework that supports your productivity and overall well-being. These tools equip you to navigate through periods of high stress with grace and efficiency, ensuring that you remain in control, no matter the pressures you face.

2.4 THE ART OF SAYING NO: SETTING BOUNDARIES FOR BETTER MENTAL HEALTH

"Boundaries are important because they create space for personal growth and self-care, as they ensure that your own emotional, mental, and physical well-being are prioritized."

— DR. CORINE WILLIAMS, PH.D.

In the mosaic of daily life, setting boundaries stands out as one of the most critical skills for maintaining mental health and enhancing productivity. Boundaries are the personal limits you set for yourself and others, and they are crucial in defining how you interact with the world. They help conserve your emotional energy, keep relationships healthy, and ensure you are not overwhelmed by demands on your time and energy. However, setting these boundaries involves learning to say no—a simple word many find incredibly difficult to articulate.

The importance of saying no cannot be overstated. It

protects your well-being by preventing burnout and stress, which often stem from over-commitment. Moreover, it allows you to prioritize better, ensuring that your time and efforts are spent on activities that align with your values and advance your goals. Despite these benefits, many hesitate to say no due to fears of offending others or missing out on opportunities. This is where the skill of saying no, politely and firmly, becomes invaluable.

When you need to decline a request, it's essential to communicate your refusal clearly and respectfully. One effective strategy is to be direct yet courteous. For instance, if a colleague asks for help on a project, but you're already overwhelmed with your workload, a response could be, "I appreciate you thinking of me for this project, but I won't be able to commit at this time due to my current work-load." This kind of response communicates your refusal clearly and shows respect for the other person's request.

Another helpful approach is to provide a *brief explanation*, which can help the requester understand your reasons without feeling dismissed. Continuing the previous example, you might add, "I need to focus on upcoming deadlines for the next few weeks." This reinforces your boundaries and allows for possible future collaboration once your schedule allows. It's essential, however, to keep your explanation brief to avoid over-justifying your decision, which can sometimes lead to the other person trying to negotiate your boundaries.

Feeling guilty for saying no is a common barrier that keeps people from setting effective boundaries. Overcoming this guilt involves recognizing that saying no is not only your right but also your responsibility to your mental health and well-being. It is essential to remember that saying no to one request allows you to say yes to other commitments— including those to your health, family, and priorities. Remind yourself that every no is an act of self-care.

Regularly evaluating your commitments is also crucial in maintaining healthy boundaries. This practice involves periodically reviewing your current obligations to see if they align with your personal and professional goals. Ask yourself whether these activities contribute to your objectives or detract from your ability to focus on what's truly important. This ongoing evaluation helps keep your commitments in check and ensures that your boundaries align with your evolving goals and priorities.

By embracing the art of saying no and setting clear boundaries, you empower yourself to manage your time and interactions more effectively. This enhances your productivity and mental well-being and improves the quality of your relationships, as it fosters mutual respect for personal limits. As you become more adept at this skill, you'll find it easier to communicate your boundaries and live a more balanced and fulfilling life.

2.5 FROM PERFECTIONISM TO PROGRESS: SHIFTING MINDSETS

 "Perfection is not attainable, but if we chase perfection, we can catch excellence."

— VINCE LOMBARDI

In our pursuit of excellence, it's easy to fall into the trap of perfectionism, where the fear of making mistakes becomes a paralyzing force that impedes progress and growth. Perfectionism often masquerades as a virtue, an admirable drive for quality and excellence. However, when left unchecked, it can lead to an endless cycle of self-criticism and missed opportunities. Understanding and mitigating the influence of perfectionist tendencies can unlock a more productive and satisfying approach to personal and professional endeavors.

The first step in overcoming perfectionism is recognizing its signs. These may vary widely among individuals, but typical indicators include a tendency to fixate on past mistakes, procrastination due to fear of failure, and an excessive preoccupation with the opinions of others regarding one's performance. You might notice these behaviors becoming more pronounced when faced with tasks that you find particularly meaningful or challenging. Acknowledging these traits is crucial as it allows you to address them consciously.

Once you've identified perfectionist tendencies, the next transformative step is to cultivate a *progress mindset*. This mindset emphasizes the value of ongoing improvement over the unattainable goal of flawless performance. Adopting a progress mindset involves appreciating that each effort you make is a step towards mastering your skills rather than a final test of your abilities. This shift can significantly reduce pressure and increase your willingness to take on challenges. For instance, rather than criticizing yourself for not perfecting a presentation, focus on what you learned from the experience and how it will improve your future presentations. This perspective fosters resilience and a more realistic appraisal of your abilities and achievements.

Setting realistic standards is another critical strategy in this journey. While high standards can motivate you to reach significant achievements, unrealistic expectations can set you up for disappointment and discouragement. Start by evaluating your current goals and expectations to see if they are attainable or need adjustment. This evaluation might mean acknowledging that some days, doing a 'good enough' job is more beneficial than pushing for perfection, which might lead to burnout. When setting new goals, make them challenging yet achievable, and ensure they align with your priorities and resources. This practical approach enhances your chances of success and keeps your motivation intact.

Celebrating imperfect successes plays a pivotal role in overcoming perfectionism. Make it a habit to recognize and celebrate your achievements, even if they aren't flawless. Every project completed, every new thing tried, and every deadline met is a victory worth acknowledging, regardless of the imperfections. These celebrations can be simple, like taking a moment to reflect on what you've accomplished or treating yourself to something you enjoy. This practice reinforces the progress mindset and helps you internalize that imperfect action is often more valuable than perfect inaction.

Through these strategies, you can start to loosen the grip of perfectionism. By recognizing its signs, promoting a mindset of progress, setting realistic standards, and celebrating all forms of success, you pave the way for a more fulfilling and less stressful life. These changes do not diminish your drive for excellence but refine it, ensuring that your pursuit of quality enhances rather than hinders your growth and happiness.

As this chapter concludes, remember that the journey from perfectionism to progress is not about lowering your standards but reframing your approach to achieving them. It's about moving from constant anxiety over possible failures to a more balanced recognition of your growth and accomplishments. This shift improves your productivity and contributes significantly to your overall well-being.

The next chapter builds on these concepts by exploring advanced mindset techniques that can further enhance personal mastery. These techniques will help consolidate the progress mindset and equip you with additional tools to manage challenges effectively, ensuring that your journey toward personal and professional growth is both successful and satisfying.

CHAPTER CHALLENGES

1. Practice the Eisenhower Box: Break your tasks into doing the urgent/important and important/non-urgent daily, and delegate the urgent/non-important and non-urgent/non-important to someone else.
2. Positive affirmation: Post 1 positive affirmation daily on your vision board or somewhere you can see it daily.

3. Breathe and focus: Before starting any task, take three deep breaths, inhaling through your nose and exhaling through your mouth.
4. Practice saying no: Look in the mirror daily and say no respectfully and politely.

CHAPTER 3: CULTIVATING DAILY HABITS FOR LONG-TERM SUCCESS

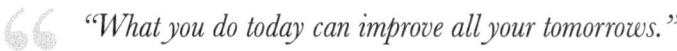 *"What you do today can improve all your tomorrows."*

— RALPH MARSTON

Imagine you are the captain of a ship embarking on a crucial voyage. Each morning, your first step is to chart the course, check the weather, and prepare your crew for the day's journey. This ritual sets the tone for the day's sailing and is crucial for a successful mission. Similarly, your morning routine is the rudder that steers your day, guiding you through the waters of daily life with intention and precision. In this chapter, we will explore how establishing a structured morning routine can transform the start of your day from chaotic or mundane to a powerful launchpad for productivity and well-being. This isn't just about waking up early; it's about waking up correctly.

3.1 THE POWER OF MORNING ROUTINES: KICKSTART YOUR DAY

 "The best dreams happen when you're awake."

— CHERIE GILDERBLOOM

Establish a Structured Start

The significance of a consistent morning routine lies in its ability to set the tone for the entire day. It's about creating a predictable and structured start that lets you take control from the outset rather than being swept away by the day's demands. This consistency significantly reduces decision fatigue, a psychological condition resulting from the burden of making too many decisions. By automating your first few activities, you conserve mental energy for more complex choices later in the day. For example, start each day with meditation, a healthy breakfast, and a review of your main tasks. In that case, you establish a baseline of calm and organization throughout your day.

Suggested Morning Activities

The activities you choose to incorporate into your morning routine can vary widely depending on your personal preferences and goals, but here are a few universally beneficial suggestions:

- **Meditation**: Starting the day with meditation can enhance your mindfulness and provide a calm, centered beginning. Five to ten minutes can significantly impact your stress levels and mental clarity.

- **Light Exercise**: Engaging in light exercise such as yoga, a brisk walk, or stretching can energize your body and increase endorphins, improving your mood and physical health.
- **Reading**: Immersing yourself in a book can stimulate your mind and provide quiet time for reflection or inspiration.
- **Planning the Day**: Reviewing your tasks and priorities can help you focus on the most important things, ensuring you manage your time effectively.

Customization Tips

Customization is vital to ensuring that your morning routine is effective but also enjoyable and sustainable. Tailor your morning activities to your personal goals and lifestyle. For instance, if physical fitness is a primary goal, emphasize exercise. When working on a project, dedicate morning time to brainstorming or planning. Aligning your routine with your personal and professional aspirations ensures that every morning contributes positively to your objectives. Additionally, consider the rhythm of your natural energy levels; some may find vigorous morning workouts invigorating, while others might prefer gentler, calmer activities to ease into the day.

Benefits of a Morning Routine

The benefits of a well-crafted morning routine extend far beyond the morning hours. Psychologically, starting your day with intention sets a proactive, rather than reactive, tone. This mindset can lead to higher productivity levels, better stress management, and greater daily control. Physically, morning routines that include exercise or healthy eating can improve energy levels, physical health, and cognitive function. Over time, the cumulative effect of these daily starts creates a foundation of discipline and self-care that enhances every aspect of your life.

By carefully designing and adhering to a morning routine, you transform the first hours of your day into a powerful catalyst for productivity, well-being, and joy. This daily commitment to starting right is not just about checking off tasks; it's about setting a daily tone of intention and accomplishment, paving the way for a complete and purposeful day. As you refine your morning routine, remember that consistency is critical—not just in execution but in continuous alignment with your evolving goals and needs. This dynamic approach ensures that your mornings continually propel you toward your desired future, making every day a stepping stone to your ultimate success.

If you want to change your world, make your bed every morning. By doing this, you will have accomplished the first thing in your day, which will encourage you to do more.

3.2 MINDFUL EATING: NUTRITION FOR THE MIND AND BODY

 "You become what you think. You are what you eat."

— BARBARA CARTLAND

Imagine savoring each bite of your meal, fully immersed in the experience, aware of the texture, the aroma, and the complex flavors dancing on your palate. This is the essence of mindful eating, a practice that transforms the simple act of eating into a profound experience that enhances your connection with food. *Mindful eating* is about engaging all your senses and paying attention to eating without distraction. It's a stark contrast to the typical scenario of mindlessly munching while glued to our screens, often leading us to overeat or miss the enjoyment of our food altogether.

The practice of mindful eating centers on the awareness of the eating experience itself, focusing on how the food makes you feel, the signals your body sends about taste and satisfaction, and the cues it gives about fullness. By eating mindfully, you not only enjoy your meals more, but you also make better nutritional choices. When you eat without distractions and truly listen to your body, you'll likely notice that foods high in sugars and fats are less satisfying and may leave you feeling sluggish. Conversely, nourishing foods provide more lasting energy and a stronger sense of satiety. This awareness can naturally lead you to make healthier choices and develop a more positive relationship with food.

Mindful eating also significantly benefits digestion. It starts with chewing your food thoroughly, an overlooked part of healthy eating habits. Chewing slowly and thoroughly helps break down the food mechanically and gives your stomach enough time to prepare for digestion, optimizing nutrient absorption and reducing digestive discomfort. Moreover, this practice helps regulate eating speed, which is crucial because it takes about 20 minutes for your brain to register fullness. Slowing down gives your body time to recognize its satiety cues, which can prevent overeating—a common issue in our fast-paced world.

Another practical step in mindful eating is to ensure that eating is your only activity during meals. In our multi-tasking society, it's common to eat while distracted. However, when you eliminate distractions and focus solely on your meal, you're more likely to notice when you are full, enjoy your food more, and digest it better, contributing to improved overall health and well-being. This single-task focus during meals can be a relaxing break from the day's hustle, offering a moment of calm and mindfulness that can enhance your mental and physical health.

Linking nutrition to mental performance further under-scores the importance of mindful eating. Like any other body part, the brain requires various nutrients to function optimally. Foods rich in antioxidants, healthy fats, vitamins, and minerals support cognitive functions such as memory, concentration, and problem-solving skills. For example, omega-3 fatty acids, found in fish like salmon and flaxseeds, are essential for brain health, playing a role in enhancing cognitive processes and emotional stability. Eating mindfully makes you more likely to select foods that nourish your body and support your mental capacities, reinforcing the critical mind-body connection that underpins overall health and wellness.

As you continue to explore and implement mindful eating, remember that it is not about perfection. It's about gradu-ally becoming more attuned to your body's experiences and needs, recognizing and respecting its signals, and making choices that enhance your health and happiness. This shift in how you approach eating can transform meals from automatic routines to moments of enjoyment and self-care, positively impacting every aspect of your life.

3.3 THE IMPACT OF PHYSICAL ACTIVITY ON MENTAL CLARITY

"The journey of a thousand miles begins with one step."

— LAO TZU

Imagine feeling more alert, focused, and at ease throughout your day. These benefits are just a few advantages that regular physical activity can bring to your mental clarity. Scientific research robustly supports the connection between the body and the mind, revealing that regular physical activity can significantly enhance cognitive functions such as memory, mood, and problem-solving abilities. When you exercise, your body increases blood flow to the brain, which can help to sharpen your alertness and make you feel more awake and ready to tackle your day. Furthermore, physical activity stimulates the production of hormones that improve mood and sleep, and it also releases proteins in the brain that can help improve the structure and function of your brain cells, leading to enhanced cognitive performance.

When considering incorporating exercise into your daily routine, thinking about various activities that can keep your body and mind engaged is beneficial. While traditional workouts like running or cycling are fantastic for boosting cardiovascular health and endurance, they're just part of the picture. Incorporating yoga into your routine, for instance, can improve flexibility and core strength, enhance mental focus, and reduce stress through its meditative elements. Walking, often overlooked, is another excellent way to incorporate movement into your day without feeling like you're committing to a heavy workout session. The rhythmic nature of walking helps clear the mind and spur creative thinking. For those seeking for more intensity, activities like martial arts or dance classes can provide exhilarating ways to improve coordination, rhythm, and cognitive agility while increasing your heart rate and using your brain to learn something new.

Developing a personal exercise plan that resonates with your lifestyle and preferences is crucial for sustainable practice. Begin by assessing your current fitness level and consider what forms of physical activity you enjoy most. Personal enjoyment is essential for consistency. Set realistic goals that motivate you without becoming overwhelmed. For example, if you are new to exercising, start with shorter, more manageable sessions a few times a week and gradually increase the duration and frequency as your stamina improves. It's also helpful to schedule your workouts as you would any other important activity; this not only ensures you allocate time for physical activity but also helps to establish it as a regular part of your routine. Remember, the goal is to find a balance where exercise feels like a natural and enjoyable part of your day, not a burdensome chore.

However, despite the best intentions, many find it challenging to maintain a routine due to common barriers such as lack of time, motivation, or resources. Overcoming these obstacles requires creative solutions and a bit of planning. For those strapped for time, consider integrating physical activity into your daily routine. For instance, take the stairs instead of the elevator, walk during your lunch break, or try at-home workout routines that can be done in under 30 minutes. Lack of motivation can be combated by setting achievable goals, tracking progress, and choosing activities you genuinely enjoy. It won't feel like a workout if you enjoy the workout. Lastly, remember that many practical exercises do not require special equipment for those concerned about resources. Activities like walking, running, and many body-weight exercises can be performed anywhere and are just as effective in promoting physical health and mental clarity.

By embracing physical activity as a vital component of your daily routine, you enhance your physical health and boost your mental well-being. The clarity, improved mood, and increased energy you gain from regular exercise can dramatically improve your quality of life, making every day more vibrant and fulfilling. As you continue to explore and integrate more physical activity into your life, remember that the most effective exercise plan you look forward to and enjoy seamlessly blends into your lifestyle and continuously enriches your body and mind.

3.4 THE IMPORTANCE OF HYDRATION IN MAINTAINING COGNITIVE HEALTH

 "Drinking water is essential to a healthy lifestyle."

— STEPHEN CURRY

Imagine your brain as a sponge; when it's dry, it becomes brittle and inefficient, but when it's hydrated, it's pliable and functional, ready to absorb and process information swiftly. This analogy is close to the truth when we consider the impact of hydration on our brain health. Dehydration, even in mild forms, can impair our cognitive functions, affecting concentration, alertness, and short-term memory. It's like trying to run a complex, resource-demanding application on a computer overheating and short on RAM; the performance drops significantly. When our brains are dehydrated, the energy production in the brain decreases, and many studies have proven that dehydration can lead to increased cortisol levels, which in turn can lead to stress.

Moreover, dehydration can lead to a reduction in brain volume, affecting brain function and structure. This shrinkage can impair activities that require attention, problem-solving, and motor coordination. Even a minimal fluid loss, such as a 2% reduction in body weight due to dehydration, which is easy to reach, especially during intense exercise or high heat, can significantly decrease cognitive performance. This level of dehydration can make tasks feel more difficult, affecting both mood and concentration levels, which can turn a regular workday into a strenuous battle against fatigue and inefficiency.

Given the critical role of hydration in brain function, ensuring optimal daily water intake is paramount. The water needed can vary based on several factors, such as age, weight, climate, and physical activity levels. However, a general rule of thumb suggested by health authorities like the Mayo Clinic advises about 3.7 liters (or about 15.5 cups) for men and 2.7 liters (about 11.5 cups) for women per day from all beverages and foods. But remember, needs can increase with exercise, high temperatures, or high altitudes. An easy way to monitor your hydration status is by looking at the color of your urine; pale yellow suggests proper hydration, while a darker color typically indicates dehydration. The human body is about 60% made of water, so my rule of thumb is to drink half your body weight in ounces. For example, if you weigh 100 pounds, drink about 50 ounces of water daily.

Integrating adequate hydration into a busy lifestyle can seem challenging, but it can be more straightforward with practical strategies. Carrying a water bottle is a concise yet effective way to ensure you always have water on hand. Investing in a reusable water bottle and keeping it within sight can be a constant reminder to drink. Numerous hydration-tracking apps can help you monitor your daily water intake and remind you to drink water at regular intervals. Setting regular reminders on your phone or computer can also be a helpful nudge to take a hydration break, which boosts your water intake and encourages you to step away from your desk, aiding mental and physical health.

The impact of other beverages on hydration and cognition is also worth noting. While water is the best source of hydration, other common drinks like coffee, tea, and even alcohol have their roles and effects. Coffee and tea, when consumed in moderation, can contribute to your daily fluid intake and offer cognitive benefits due to their caffeine content, which has been shown to enhance brain function, improving mood, reaction time, and memory. However, it's crucial to moderate your intake, as excessive caffeine can lead to dehydration and sleep disturbances. Alcohol, on the other hand, is a diuretic, which means it increases the body's production of urine, leading to a loss of fluids and electrolytes that are essential for normal brain function. Moderate alcohol consumption can have some cognitive benefits in older adults, but excessive drinking is detrimental to mental health and can exacerbate dehydration.

By understanding the vital role of hydration in cognitive performance and mood and implementing strategies to maintain optimal hydration, you can support your brain's health and enhance your mental capacities. Whether by increasing your water intake, moderating other beverages, or using technology to stay on track, small changes in your hydration habits can significantly affect your cognitive function and overall well-being.

3.5 THE IMPORTANCE OF SLEEP: RESTORATIVE PRACTICES FOR THE MIND

"Sleep is an investment in the energy you need to be effective tomorrow."

— TOM ROTH

Sleep is not merely a pause in our daily routines but a critical restoration period that our brains and bodies require to function optimally. During sleep, your brain engages in highly orchestrated processes vital for memory consolidation, emotional regulation, and maintaining cognitive functions. This nightly reset allows your brain to process new information, store it effectively, and remove toxins accumulated during the day. When you learn something new, it's during sleep that the neural connections strengthening that knowledge are most actively formed and reinforced. This consolidation process is crucial for learning new information, stabilizing mood, and enhancing overall cognitive function.

To optimize these benefits, adhering to good sleep hygiene practices is essential. Establishing a regular sleep schedule by going to bed and waking up at the same time each day sets your body's internal clock to expect rest at a particular hour, making it easier to fall asleep and wake up naturally. Creating a restful environment is equally important. Your bedroom should be a sanctuary designed for sleep, which means keeping it cool, quiet, and dark. Invest in a good quality mattress and pillows to support a comfortable night's sleep, and consider blackout curtains or an eye mask to block out light.

Additionally, the hour leading up to bedtime should be a wind-down period. Avoiding stimulants like caffeine and nicotine close to bedtime is crucial, as they can disrupt sleep patterns. Similarly, while technology has become a staple in our lives, the blue light emitted by screens can interfere with the production of melatonin, the hormone that signals your brain it's time to sleep. Try reading a book or practicing relaxation exercises instead of scrolling through your phone right before bed.

Despite our best efforts, we will eventually encounter sleep challenges such as insomnia or disrupted sleep patterns. Addressing these issues requires more than good sleep hygiene alone. For those struggling with insomnia, it's essential to focus on natural methods and lifestyle adjustments initially. Regular physical activity can promote better sleep, helping to fall asleep faster and enjoy deeper sleep. However, timing is vital;

exercising too close to bedtime can have the opposite effect. Managing stress is also crucial, as it is often a primary cause of sleep disturbances. Techniques such as mindfulness meditation, deep breathing exercises, and yoga can reduce stress and improve sleep quality. Maintaining a sleep diary can be helpful for disrupted sleep. Tracking your sleep patterns and habits can identify behaviors detrimental to sleep quality. If self-help methods don't resolve your sleep issues, it may be time to consult a healthcare provider to discuss other treatments.

The impact of sleep on daily functioning is profound. Adequate sleep can enhance your productivity, mood, and decision-making abilities. With sufficient rest, you are more likely to have better concentration and memory throughout the day, which can improve job performance and interpersonal interactions. On the emotional front, good sleep has been linked to better mood regulation and a lower likelihood of depression and anxiety. The reason lies in sleep's ability to help regulate the hormones that affect our emotions, including cortisol, the stress hormone. When well-rested, your body can manage these hormonal balances more effectively, improving overall emotional stability.

Understanding and implementing these practices can improve sleep quality, enhancing overall health and well-being. Remember, sleep is a foundational element of health, just as critical as diet and exercise. Prioritizing good sleep is prioritizing your long-term health and daily effectiveness. Ensuring you get enough restorative sleep each night improves your nights and every part of your day.

3.6 DAILY JOURNALING: YOUR THOUGHTS IN WRITING

 "Journal writing, when it becomes a ritual for transformation, is not only life-changing but life-expanding."

— JENNIFER WILLIAMSON

Journaling is a uniquely personal and powerful practice in the tapestry of self-improvement tools. It is a mirror reflecting your inner world, capturing thoughts and emotions and unraveling them, making sense of what lies beneath the surface. Journaling is far more than just writing down what you did each day; it's a ritual of self-reflection that can decrease stress, enhance creativity, and deepen your understanding of your narrative. When you commit your thoughts to paper, you're not merely recording your experiences but actively engaging with them, parsing through your reactions, and gaining clarity on your feelings.

Journaling can be particularly effective in managing stress. It acts as a form of stress relief by allowing you to express your thoughts and emotions in a safe, private space. This expression can be therapeutic, as it often provides a release of bottled-up emotions and stress, offering a feeling of relief and lightness. For many, writing helps organize thoughts that may feel chaotic or overwhelming in the mind. By laying them out on paper, you can approach your challenges more systematically and reduce the anxiety they cause. Furthermore, the reflective nature of writing can lead to greater self-awareness and insight, helping you identify sources of stress and uncover patterns in your thoughts and behaviors that may contribute to your distress.

Beyond stress reduction, journaling is a potent tool for boosting creativity. It provides a playground for your thoughts, where wild ideas can be explored without judgment. *Free writing*, in particular, allows you to bypass the inner critic that stifles creative thought, enabling a free flow of ideas. This technique involves writing continuously for a set period without worrying about spelling, grammar, or making sense. The practice ignites creativity and builds a bridge to deeper subconscious insights, often leading to novel solutions and innovative ideas that may not surface through more conventional thinking processes.

To integrate journaling into your daily routine effectively, consider it a ritual as integral to your well-being as eating or sleeping. Establishing a specific time and place for journaling can help make this practice a regular part of your life. The morning might be ideal for setting intentions and planning the day, while evenings could be better suited for reflective writing on the day's events and emotions. Your environment should be comfortable and conducive to introspection—quiet, personal, and interruptions-free. Whether it's a cozy corner of your bedroom, a peaceful outdoor setting, or a dedicated space in your home office, the right environment can significantly enhance the quality of your journaling experience.

Numerous anecdotal accounts illustrate the profound impact of journaling on personal development and mental clarity. Consider the story of Emily, a project manager struggling with burnout and low job satisfaction. Through daily journaling, Emily began to understand the root causes of her dissatisfaction: a lack of creative expression and autonomy in her work. This insight was pivotal. It led her to negotiate a new role within her company that offered more innovative projects and independence, dramatically improving her job satisfaction and overall happiness.

Similarly, Mark, a retired veteran, used journaling to cope with his transition to civilian life. His entries helped him process his experiences and emotions, eventually leading him to discover a passion for teaching. He now uses his skills and experiences to teach leadership courses at a community college, finding new purpose and joy in helping others grow.

These stories highlight how journaling can enrich your life, providing clarity and direction. As you explore the different techniques and make journaling a part of your daily routine, you may find that it not only helps you navigate the complexities of life but also becomes a cherished space for self-expression and discovery, a personal sanctuary where you can confront your truths, celebrate your successes, and continually evolve towards the person you aspire to be.

3.7 CONTINUOUS LEARNING: KEEPING YOUR MIND ACTIVE

 "Once you stop learning, you start dying."

— ALBERT EINSTEIN

In an age where change is the only constant, the ability to keep learning and adapting is not just an advantage but a necessity. Continuous learning is the fuel that keeps the engine of your mind running efficiently, ensuring you remain competitive in your career and fulfilled in your endeavors. Embracing lifelong learning helps keep your cognitive abilities sharp, enhances your problem-solving skills, and even delays the mental decline associated with aging.

Lifelong learning encompasses a broad spectrum of activities contributing to continuous personal and professional development. These could range from acquiring new skills to updating old ones to exploring new areas of knowledge. The beauty of learning as an adult is that it is mainly self-directed and goal-oriented. You choose what new knowledge or skills to pursue based on your interests and needs, which enhances the learning experience, making it more relevant and enjoyable.

The resources available for learning today are vast and more accessible than ever. Online courses, for instance, offer flexibility and a wide range of subjects. Platforms like Coursera, Udemy, or Khan Academy provide courses on everything from philosophy to data science, many of which are taught by leading experts worldwide. Workshops, seminars, and webinars are also invaluable resources, offering more personalized and interactive learning experiences. Moreover, books—whether in print, digital, or audio format—remain among the most profound sources of knowledge. Podcasts, too, have surged in popularity as a tool for learning, providing insights and information in convenient, digestible segments that you can listen to during a commute or while exercising.

Incorporating learning into everyday life is about creating habits that encourage knowledge acquisition without overwhelming your daily schedule. One effective strategy is to dedicate daily or weekly time to educational activities. This could be as simple as reading a book chapter each night, listening to a podcast during your morning run, or setting aside an hour every weekend to progress through an online course. Another powerful approach is to engage with others who share similar learning interests. Discussion groups, whether in person or online, can enhance understanding and retention of information. They provide diverse perspectives and insights, which can deepen your knowledge and make learning more engaging and less isolating.

The benefits of maintaining an active mind through continuous learning are substantial. Professionally, it keeps you current in your field, making you a more attractive candidate for promotions and career opportunities. It can also pivot you into new careers as you acquire new skills that open up new possibilities. Learning new things can be incredibly satisfying. It feeds your curiosity and can significantly improve your quality of life by providing a sense of accomplishment and purpose. Moreover, the adaptability and resilience that come from being a lifelong learner are invaluable in navigating modern life's complexities and rapid changes.

As this chapter closes, reflect on how continuous learning has shaped or could shape your personal and professional life. Consider the resources and strategies discussed and how you might integrate them into your routine. By making learning a continuous part of your life, you enhance your capabilities and contribute to a broader culture of knowledge and growth. This commitment to lifelong learning is not just about personal or professional development; it's about enriching your life experience, ensuring you remain vibrant, curious, and engaged, no matter your challenges.

The next chapter will build on these concepts and explore advanced personal and professional growth strategies. As you continue to expand your knowledge and skills, remember that each step forward enriches your own life and the lives of those around you, weaving your personal growth into the larger fabric of community and societal advancement.

CHAPTER CHALLENGES

1. Morning routine: Start with a 5-minute walk daily and eventually build up to 30 minutes.
2. Mindful eating: Start by eating at least one serving of fruit or vegetable daily. Eat it slowly, chewing each bite for 20 chews. Eventually, build up to eating seven servings of fruit or vegetables daily.
3. Water intake: Start measuring and tracking your water intake daily with an app or a water canteen, and within six months, you should be able to drink half your body weight in ounces.
4. Winding down: Set an alarm at the same time each day to shut down screens, wind down for bed, and be in bed within the next hour.

CHAPTER 4: DEVELOPING EMOTIONAL INTELLIGENCE AND RESILIENCE

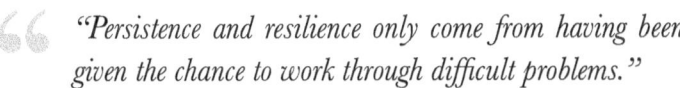

"Persistence and resilience only come from having been given the chance to work through difficult problems."

— GEVER TULLEY

I magine navigating through your day with a profound understanding of your emotions and those of the people around you, turning every interaction into an opportunity for personal and relational growth. This isn't just a skill reserved for the select few; it's an attainable asset known as emotional intelligence (EI). This chapter delves into the essence of EI, breaking down its components, illustrating its impact on personal and professional success, and providing practical tools for its assessment and enhancement. As you explore these insights, you'll discover how cultivating emotional intelligence can transform challenges into stepping stones toward a more fulfilled life.

4.1 UNDERSTANDING EMOTIONAL INTELLIGENCE: THE BASICS

 "Emotional intelligence is your ability to recognize and understand emotions in yourself and others, and your ability to use this awareness to manage your behavior and relationships."

— TRAVIS BRADBERRY

Define Emotional Intelligence (EI)

Emotional intelligence is the capacity to be aware of, control, express one's emotions, and to handle interpersonal relationships judiciously and empathetically. This skill allows you to recognize and understand your emotional states and those of others and use this awareness to manage your behavior and relationships more effectively. EI is not just about emotional awareness; it's about using that knowledge to create positive outcomes in both personal and professional contexts. For instance, it enables you to anticipate and better manage your reactions in stressful situations or to resolve conflicts by understanding the perspectives and emotional states of others involved.

Components of EI

Emotional intelligence can be broken down into two primary competencies: personal and social competence. *Personal competence* is composed of self-awareness and self-management. Self-awareness involves understanding your emotions, strengths, weaknesses, drives, and goals and recognizing their impact on others. Self-management refers to your ability to control impulsive feelings and behaviors, manage your emotions healthily, take initiative, follow through on commitments, and adapt to changing circumstances. *Social competence* encompasses social awareness and relationship management. Social awareness allows you to understand other people's emotions, needs, concerns, pick up on emotional cues, feel socially comfortable, and recognize the power dynamics in a group or organization. Relationship management involves:

- Developing and maintaining good relationships.
- Communicating clearly.
- Inspiring and influencing others.
- Working well in a team.
- Managing conflict.

EI and Personal Success

The impact of emotional intelligence on personal success is profound. In the workplace, high EI contributes to better teamwork, more decisive leadership, and increased productivity. It enhances your ability to work under pressure, facilitates conflict resolution, and fosters relationships with colleagues, which can advance your career. In personal relationships, emotional intelligence helps build deeper connections, fosters emotional support, promotes mutual understanding, and enhancing relationship satisfaction. Furthermore, individuals with high emotional intelligence are generally more resilient; they can navigate stress and setbacks more effectively, maintaining a positive outlook despite challenges.

Assessing Your EI

First, you must assess your EI levels to enhance your emotional intelligence. This can be achieved through various methods, including self-assessment questionnaires and 360-degree feedback tools. Self-assessment tools typically ask you to rate your behavior in areas that reflect key EI competencies, such as empathy, emotional regulation, and social skills. These assessments can provide insights into which areas of EI you need to develop further. However, self-assessments are often limited by one's self-awareness level. To counteract this, 360-degree feedback tools can be used. These tools involve collecting feedback about your emotional competencies from people at all levels of your organization—supervisors, peers, subordinates—and a self-evaluation. The feedback provides a more objective view of your EI, highlighting discrepancies between how you see yourself and how others perceive you. This comprehensive approach aids in accurately assessing your EI and pinpoints specific areas for improvement.

By understanding the foundations of emotional intelligence and assessing your EI competencies, you are better equipped to navigate the complexities of emotional interactions in your personal and professional environments. This knowledge provides a stepping stone towards cultivating a richer, more understanding, and practical existence, enhancing every aspect of your life by transforming how you connect with the world.

4.2 TECHNIQUES FOR ENHANCING EMPATHY AND SOCIAL SKILLS

 "The great gift of human beings is that we have the power of empathy, we can all sense a mysterious connection to each other."

— MERYL STREEP

Empathy and social skills are indispensable tools in your personal and professional life. They are bridges connecting us to others in meaningful ways. Developing these skills can significantly enhance your interactions and relationships, making your social experiences more rewarding and effective. Let's explore practical steps to enhance empathy and refine your social skills, ensuring you're not just present in your interactions but actively contribute to their richness and depth.

Developing Empathy

Empathy is the ability to understand and share another person's feelings from their perspective. It goes beyond sympathy, which is compassion for someone; empathy involves a more profound connection that can lead to more effective communication and stronger relationships. One effective way to enhance empathy is through *active listening*, which means fully concentrating on what is being said rather than passively hearing the speaker. This practice involves listening with all senses and giving your full attention to the speaker without planning your response while the other person is talking. Active listening also includes reflecting on what you have heard and asking questions to clarify your understanding, which helps comprehend the speaker's perspective and shows that you genuinely care about their feelings and experiences.

Another technique to develop empathy is *perspective-taking*, which involves putting yourself in another person's shoes. This can be practiced by imagining how you would feel about the other person's situation or by asking them to share their feelings and experiences. Engaging in this practice helps you understand why others may feel or react in specific ways, which can be particularly useful in resolving conflicts and building closer relationships. Additionally, practicing compassion plays a crucial role in empathy. This involves recognizing another person's emotional state, feeling moved by their suffering, and taking action to help alleviate it. Compassion can be practiced through small acts of kindness, thoughtful gestures, or simply offering support and understanding someone in need.

Improving Social Skills

Practical social skills are vital in navigating the complexities of interpersonal relationships and professional networks. They involve more than just conversational abilities; they include non-verbal communication, such as body language and eye contact, which can often speak louder than words. To elevate your social skills, start by focusing on your non-verbal cues. Pay attention to the signals you're sending through your body language, such as crossing your arms or avoiding eye contact, which might be interpreted as disinterest or discomfort. Instead, adopt a more open posture and maintain eye contact to convey engagement and confidence.

Effective communication is another critical aspect of social skills. This means speaking clearly and concisely and being mindful of your tone and words' impact on others. Practice expressing yourself honestly and respectfully, being careful to avoid language that could be perceived as aggressive or dismissive. Additionally, being attentive to non-verbal cues in others can help you better understand their reactions and feelings, allowing you to adjust your approach accordingly. This can be particularly useful in group settings where dynamics constantly shift, and being attuned to these changes can guide your interactions.

Role-Playing Scenarios

Role-playing exercises are a practical and effective way to practice and refine your empathy and social skills. These scenarios allow you to experiment with different approaches to handling various social situations in a controlled environment. For example, you might role-play a scenario where you must deliver difficult feedback to a colleague or navigate a sensitive conversation with a friend. You can explore different strategies for communicating effectively, managing emotions, and responding to feedback through role-playing. This helps build your confidence and provides insights into what works best in various situations based on real-time feedback from others involved in the exercise.

Empathy in Diverse Settings

In today's globalized world, the ability to exercise empathy across diverse cultural and social contexts is more important than ever. This involves recognizing and respecting cultural differences, which can influence how emotions are expressed and understood. Developing cultural empathy can help prevent misunderstandings and improve interactions with individuals from different backgrounds. This can be particularly valuable in professional settings where you may work with colleagues, clients, or customers worldwide. To enhance your cultural empathy, try to learn about other cultures, ask respectful questions, and be open to learning from the experiences of others. This enriches your personal experiences and enhances your professional capabilities, making you a more effective and compassionate communicator across various social and cultural contexts.

By actively engaging in these practices, you enhance your ability to connect with others more meaningfully and equip yourself with the tools to navigate the social complexities of your personal and professional life. Whether through strengthening your listening skills, practicing empathy, or refining your social interactions, the journey towards enhanced social skills and empathy is a rewarding pursuit that promises to enrich your relationships and broaden your understanding of the world around you.

4.3 BUILDING RESILIENCE: OVERCOMING ADVERSITY WITH GRACE

> *"Every adversity, every failure, every heartache carries with it the seed of an equal or greater benefit."*

> — NAPOLEON HILL

Resilience is often likened to the robustness of certain materials that, no matter how much they're twisted or stretched, return to their original shape. For humans, resilience isn't about returning to a previous state but rather the capacity to endure life's challenges and emerge perhaps altered but undeniably more vital. This ability to bounce back from setbacks and adapt to challenging circumstances isn't just an innate quality possessed by a fortunate few; it's a skill that can be developed and honed through deliberate practice and mindset shifts.

One key trait shared by resilient individuals is optimism. This isn't about wearing rose-colored glasses or dismissing the gravity of situations. Instead, it's about maintaining a hopeful outlook that focuses on potential solutions rather than dwelling solely on the problems. This optimism fuels resilience, providing the emotional buoyancy needed to navigate turmoil. Another crucial trait is having a solid support network. Relationships that provide emotional, informational, and practical support can be lifelines during challenging times, offering assistance and a sense of belonging and purpose. Additionally, resilient people view failures as valuable feedback rather than evidence of incompetence. This perspective shift transforms setbacks into learning opportunities, fostering a mindset more about growth than proving worth.

To build resilience, it's vital to set realistic goals. These should be challenging enough to push you but achievable enough to avoid constant frustration. Goal setting acts as a roadmap through adversity, providing clear markers of progress and helping maintain motivation. Alongside goal setting, nurturing a positive self-image is essential. This involves recognizing your strengths and accomplishments and treating yourself with compassion rather than harsh judgment. This self-compassion reinforces your belief in your capabilities, which is crucial in times of doubt and setbacks.

Maintaining a hopeful outlook is another actionable tip for building resilience. Hope is not just a feel-good emotion; it's a dynamic cognitive motivational system. According to researchers, hope involves *pathways thinking*, finding routes to your desired goals, and agency thinking, the motivational drive to use those routes. To cultivate hope, focus on planning steps towards your goals and visualize yourself achieving them. This visualization boosts your emotional state and clarifies the steps needed to succeed.

Challenges and setbacks are inevitable parts of life, but each offers a unique opportunity for growth. Viewing adversity through this lens can significantly change your reaction to it. When faced with setbacks, instead of reacting with despair or frustration, ask yourself what can be learned from this experience. This could involve seeking feedback on what didn't work, reflecting on personal missteps, and planning how to avoid similar issues. For instance, if a project at work didn't go as planned, analyze the factors that led to the result instead of brooding over the failure. Were there unforeseen variables? Did you need additional resources or skills? Understanding these elements can transform a setback into a stepping stone toward future success.

This approach to building resilience—setting realistic goals, nurturing a positive self-image, maintaining a hopeful outlook, and learning from setbacks—creates a robust framework for dealing with life's inevitable ups and downs. By actively developing these traits and strategies, you equip yourself with the tools to survive challenges and thrive despite them. As you continue to strengthen your resilience, remember that each challenge is not just an obstacle to be endured but an opportunity to enhance your understanding, expand your capabilities, and deepen your appreciation of life's complexities.

4.4 THE ROLE OF MINDFULNESS IN EMOTIONAL REGULATION

 "Training your mind to be in the present moment is the number one key to making healthier choices."

— SUSAN ALBERS

Mindfulness, which echoes through contemporary psychology and wellness corridors, is fundamentally about cultivating a profound presence in the moment. This practice involves a heightened awareness of your current thoughts, feelings, and surroundings, approached without judgment or distraction. Think of mindfulness as tuning into a radio frequency where the static noise of life's distractions fades away, allowing you to experience the clarity of direct reception. This mental state of increased awareness and focus enhances your ability to navigate the intricacies of your emotions and the world around you.

Exploring basic mindfulness techniques can serve as your toolkit for achieving this state of mental clarity and emotional stability. *Focused breathing*, for instance, is a cornerstone of mindfulness practice that involves paying close attention to the breath. This technique draws your attention away from distracting thoughts and centers it on the rhythm of your breathing, which naturally slows down the heartbeat and induces a calm state. Mindful meditation extends this by scanning your body for tension or discomfort, acknowledging these feelings without attempting to change them, and gently guiding your focus back to your breath. These practices help calm the mind and sharpen your focus, making you more attuned to the subtleties of your emotional landscape.

Body scans are another effective mindfulness exercise, particularly useful in identifying and managing emotions that manifest physically. By mentally scanning your body from head to toe, you consciously acknowledge areas of physical tension or discomfort, often linked to emotional stress. This technique promotes relaxation and enhances awareness of how emotions affect your body, providing insights crucial for emotional regulation. Regular practice of these mindfulness techniques cultivates a deeper, more intuitive understanding of your emotional triggers and responses, fostering a balanced mental state that enhances your ability to cope with stress and anxiety.

The benefits of mindfulness extend significantly into the realm of emotional health. By decreasing reactivity, mindfulness allows you to respond to situations with consideration rather than an impulsive approach. This can be particularly beneficial in high-stress environments, where your instinct might be to react without thought. Additionally, mindfulness increases patience by slowing the mind's tendency to jump to conclusions or react based on incomplete information. This can lead to more thoughtful interactions with others and a more measured approach to problem-solving. Over time, mindfulness fosters a general sense of emotional stability, not by eliminating negative emotions but changing your relationship with them. You begin to see these emotions as transient states rather than defining aspects of your identity, which diminishes their impact and allows you to remain composed even in challenging circumstances.

Incorporating mindfulness into your daily life can transform ordinary activities into emotional regulation and self-awareness exercises. Simple actions like mindful eating, where you focus entirely on the eating experience, appreciating the textures and flavors of your food, can turn a routine meal into a mindfulness practice. Similarly, engaging in mindful walking—being fully present with each step, noticing the feel of the ground under your feet, the surrounding sounds, and the rhythm of your breathing—can transform a simple walk into a rejuvenating practice that enhances your mindfulness skills. These activities do not require extra time; they need a shift in how you approach everyday tasks, turning them into opportunities for mindfulness practice.

As you weave mindfulness into your daily routines, you equip yourself with a powerful tool that enhances your emotional intelligence, bolsters your mental health, and enriches your interactions with the world. This ongoing practice deepens your understanding of yourself and enhances your capacity to engage more meaningfully and rationally with life.

4.5 STRESS MANAGEMENT TECHNIQUES THAT WORK

 "The greatest weapon against stress is our ability to choose one thought over another."

— WILLIAM JAMES

In today's fast-paced world, stress can often feel like an unavoidable side effect of trying to keep up, whether meeting professional deadlines, managing personal relationships, or navigating daily responsibilities. However, managing stress effectively is crucial for maintaining your well-being and protecting your long-term health and happiness. By identifying your unique stressors, employing effective stress reduction techniques, and creating a personalized stress management plan, you can transform your approach to handling stress, turning potential overwhelm into manageable challenges.

Identifying your stressors is the first critical step toward effective stress management. This involves closely examining the situations, relationships, or activities that consistently trigger stress reactions. These triggers can be as varied as a high-pressure job, financial worries, or personal relationships. Recognizing these elements helps you understand the patterns of your stress responses and lays the groundwork for addressing them effectively. For instance, if deadlines at work consistently cause anxiety, you might pinpoint poor time management or a fear of inadequate performance as underlying issues. Similarly, if personal relationships are a source of stress, it might be due to unresolved conflicts or unrealistic expectations from one or both parties involved. Understanding these triggers isn't about placing blame but recognizing the factors contributing to your stress so you can address them constructively.

Once you've identified your stressors, exploring various stress reduction techniques can help you find the best strategies. Exercise, for example, is a widely recommended method for reducing stress. Physical activity helps release endorphins, the body's natural mood elevators, which can alleviate feelings of stress and anxiety. Whether it's a brisk walk, a run, or a yoga session, finding a form of exercise you enjoy can significantly affect your ability to manage stress. Relaxation methods such as deep breathing exercises, meditation, or progressive muscle relaxation are also effective in calming the mind and reducing the physical symptoms of stress. These practices help slow your heart rate, reduce blood pressure, and promote a sense of calm and control. Effective time management is also crucial in preventing the stress that comes from feeling like you're constantly behind schedule or out of control. Techniques such as prioritizing tasks, breaking projects into smaller steps, and using planning tools can help you manage your time more effectively and reduce stress.

Creating a personal stress management plan involves integrating the stress reduction techniques that work best for you into a structured approach tailored to your lifestyle and stressors. This plan might include setting aside specific times each day for relaxation practices, scheduling regular exercise, and developing a time management strategy that helps you handle your professional and personal responsibilities without becoming overwhelmed. Additionally, your plan should include regular check-ins where you assess your stress levels and the effectiveness of your management strategies. This ongoing evaluation allows you to make adjustments as needed, ensuring that your stress management techniques continue to meet your needs over time.

The long-term benefits of effective stress management are extensive. Not only does it improve your immediate well-being, but it also has profound health benefits that can enhance your quality of life. Regularly managing stress reduces the risk of chronic conditions such as heart disease, obesity, and depression. It also helps preserve cognitive function and can increase your lifespan. Beyond these physical health benefits, effective stress management contributes to better emotional health, improving mood, boosting energy levels, and enhancing overall satisfaction. By taking proactive steps to manage stress, you're investing in a healthier, more fulfilling future, equipped to handle whatever challenges come your way with resilience and confidence.

4.6 CRISIS MANAGEMENT: MAINTAINING YOUR COOL IN TOUGH TIMES

"If you keep your cool, you'll get everything."

— ELLIOTT ERWITT

When unexpected crises strike, the immediate response can significantly influence the outcome. Maintaining composure under pressure isn't just about staying calm; it's about strategically navigating through the storm with precision and foresight. One effective strategy is staying informed. Knowledge is a powerful tool in crisis management. Having up-to-date, accurate information lets you make informed decisions rather than reactive guesses. This involves identifying reliable sources of information and continually updating your understanding of the situation as it evolves.

Another crucial strategy is to focus on controllable aspects. Certain elements will be beyond your control in any crisis. Spending your energy fretting about these aspects can lead to increased anxiety and ineffective crisis management. Instead, identify what you can control and direct your efforts there. This approach enhances your effectiveness and contributes to a sense of agency, reducing feelings of helplessness.

Additionally, practicing calmness is vital. This doesn't mean suppressing your emotions; it involves acknowledging your feelings but responding to them in a way that keeps you level-headed. Techniques such as deep breathing, mindfulness, or even brief physical exercises can help manage physiological symptoms of stress, aiding in maintaining a calm demeanor.

Preparing emotionally for potential crises is equally important. *Scenario planning* is a valuable tool here. This involves thinking through possible crisis scenarios and planning your responses. Such preparation helps anticipate the decisions you might need to make and reduces the likelihood of being caught off guard. *Mental rehearsal,* where you visualize yourself handling a crisis calmly and effectively, can also enhance your emotional readiness. This technique, often used by athletes and public speakers, helps condition your mind to respond to actual crises more effectively.

Building and relying on a support network during crises cannot be overstated. Whether it's colleagues, friends, family, or professional counselors, having a support network provides emotional relief and practical assistance. Professional help, such as therapists or crisis counselors, can be precious in providing expert guidance and strategies tailored to the specific nature of the crisis. This support helps you navigate the situation more effectively and safeguards your mental health during challenging times.

After a crisis, the *recovery phase* is critical. This involves both emotional and practical steps to return to normalcy. Prioritizing mental health is crucial. Engage in activities that promote emotional healing, such as talking about your experiences, seeking therapy, or engaging in stress-reducing practices like yoga or meditation. Practically, it may involve rebuilding what was lost or establishing new routines that accommodate the crises' changes. The recovery phase is not just about returning to how things were but learning from the experience and emerging stronger and more prepared for future challenges.

Navigating through crises with grace involves a combination of preparedness, strategic thinking, and emotional intelligence. You can manage crises by staying informed, focusing on what you can control, preparing emotionally, relying on your support network, and taking deliberate steps toward recovery. These strategies help deal with immediate challenges and build resilience, equipping you with the skills to handle future crises more confidently and effectively.

As we wrap up this discussion on crisis management, remember that the principles outlined here extend beyond navigating crises; they are essential components of living a resilient, proactive life. These practices prepare you to face unexpected challenges and embrace the growth opportunities that come with them. The next chapter will explore how these strategies integrate into broader life practices, enhancing your ability to manage crises, everyday stress, and challenges. This seamless integration empowers you to lead a life of resilience, growth, and stability.

CHAPTER CHALLENGES

1. Emotional Intelligence (EI): Find your *emotional intelligence quotient* by taking a self-assessment test online and typing "emotional intelligence test" into any search engine.
2. Realistic goal: Set a realistic goal in your career, life, family, or health. Write down the steps to achieve that goal.
3. Body scan: Spend at least 5 minutes daily scanning your body from head to toe, acknowledging any tension or discomfort and relaxing those areas.
4. Reduce stress: Find a way to reduce stress with something you enjoy, whether exercising or meditation. Do it daily for at least 20 minutes.

CHANGE SOMEONE'S WORLD

To Give is to Live

"Helping one person might not change the whole world, but it could change the world for one person"

— UNKNOWN

People who give without expectation live longer, happier successful lives.

To make that happen, I ask you…

Would you help someone you've never met, even if you never get acknowledged for it?

Who is this person? They're like you. Or, at least, like you used to be. Less wisdom, feeling stuck, struggling, and need help, but not sure where to look.

I aim to make transforming the mind for success for anyone and the only way for me to accomplish that is by reaching everyone.

This is where you come in. Most people do, in fact, judge a book by its cover and its reviews. So, here's my ask on behalf of a struggling person trying to transform and improve their life you've never met:

Please help that person seeking personal growth and practical action steps by leaving this book a review.

On audible - tap the three dots in the upper right-hand corner, click rate and review, and then leave a few sentences of what you like with a star rating.

On a Kindle or e-reader, scroll to the bottom of the book and swipe up. It will prompt a review for you.

These functions change occasionally. If you can't find how to leave a review in these formats, you can always go to the book page on Amazon or wherever you bought this book and leave a review on the page.

Your gift cost no money, but can change a person's life forever. Your review could help...

- ...one more person provide for their family.
- ...one more entrepreneur get to the next mile stone.
- ...one more employee find an awesome job.
- ...one more client transform their life.
- ...one dream come true.

To get that 'feel good' feeling and help this person, all you have to do is...leave a review which takes 60 seconds.

If you feel good about helping someone that feels stuck, you are my kind of person.

I'm that much more excited to help you achieve success faster than you can possibly imagine. You'll love the transformative strategies I'm about to share in the coming chapters.

Thank you. Now, back to transforming the mind.

- To transforming your mind, DK Kang

P.S. If you provide something of value to another person, it makes you more valuable to them. If you're getting value from this book and believe someone else will benefit from it, then send this book their way.

CHAPTER 5: ENHANCING INTERPERSONAL RELATIONSHIPS THROUGH MINDSET

 "Every interpersonal situation has a solution in which everyone wins."

— DEL CLOSE

I magine stepping into a room full of strangers or sitting across from a loved one equipped with the invisible yet powerful tool of active listening. This skill, often overlooked, is the key that unlocks deeper connections, allowing you not just to hear but genuinely understand those around you. This chapter delves into active listening, a fundamental aspect of building more robust, meaningful relationships. By mastering this skill, you transform every interaction, ensuring you are not merely a conversation participant but a catalyst for greater understanding and mutual respect.

5.1 ACTIVE LISTENING SKILLS FOR DEEPER CONNECTIONS

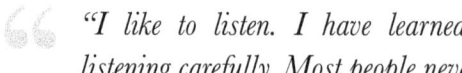

"I like to listen. I have learned a great deal from listening carefully. Most people never listen."

— ERNEST HEMINGWAY

Understanding Active Listening

Active listening is a dynamic process that involves fully concentrating, understanding, responding thoughtfully, and remembering what is being said. Unlike *passive hearing*, which is the involuntary act of perceiving sound, active listening requires deliberate effort. It's about engaging with the speaker verbally and non-verbally—through affirming sounds, nodding, and maintaining eye contact—to signal that you are fully present and genuinely interested in their words. This level of engagement enhances communication and strengthens relationships by demonstrating respect and validation for the speaker's thoughts and feelings.

Techniques for Better Listening

Several practical techniques can enhance your listening skills. *Mirroring*, for example, involves subtly mimicking the speaker's body language, which can create a sense of empathy and rapport. This does not mean copying every gesture or movement but rather reflecting a similar posture or facial expression, which conveys that you agree with the speaker. Another powerful technique is *paraphrasing*. You show that you actively engage with their message by restating what the speaker has said in your own words. This confirms that you have understood the content and allows any miscommunications to be clarified. Additionally, asking open-ended questions can deepen the conversation. These questions encourage the speaker to elaborate on their thoughts and share more detailed information, which can lead to more prosperous and more meaningful exchanges.

Barriers to Effective Listening

Despite its importance, several barriers can impede effective listening. *Distractions*, external like noises or internal, like wandering thoughts, can disrupt focus. To overcome these, it is crucial to consciously direct your attention to the speaker by moving to a quieter location or setting aside distracting thoughts until later. *Biases and preconceived notions* can also hinder listening. If you enter a conversation with predetermined judgments about the speaker or their topic, you are less likely to engage with their actual words fully. Recognizing and setting aside these biases as much as possible allows you to hear and understand perspectives different from your own.

Benefits of Active Listening

The benefits of active listening extend far beyond the conversation at hand. It fosters deeper connections by building trust and respect, foundational elements of any strong relationship. When people feel heard, they are more likely to open up and share more honestly and freely, reducing misunderstandings and conflicts. Furthermore, active listening enhances your ability to absorb and remember information, improving your interactions personally and professionally. Whether you are dealing with a friend expressing a problem, a partner discussing their feelings, or a colleague explaining a complex project, your ability to listen actively can significantly influence the effectiveness of your response and the strength of your relationships.

Active listening is more than a skill; it is an investment in your relationships and a commitment to understanding others. Practicing and refining your listening abilities ensures your connections are maintained and strengthened. Each conversation becomes an opportunity to foster greater intimacy and understanding, paving the way for more robust and supportive relationships. Through active listening, you become a better friend, partner, colleague, and leader who hears what others are saying and responds with empathy and insight. As we explore other facets of interpersonal relationships in this chapter, remember the power of active listening as a fundamental tool in your relationship-building toolkit.

5.2 CONFLICT RESOLUTION: FINDING COMMON GROUND

> *"Peace is not the absence of conflict; it is the ability to handle conflict by peaceful means."*
>
> — RONALD REAGAN

In any relationship, be it personal or professional, conflicts are inevitable. They stem from differences in perspectives, goals, or values. Understanding the different styles of conflict resolution and identifying your default approach can significantly affect how you manage and resolve these conflicts. Broadly, there are five recognized styles: accommodating, avoiding, collaborating, competing, and compromising. Each style has its place and effectiveness depending on the situation and the relationship dynamics. For instance, *accommodating* might work well when the relationship is more valuable than the conflict. Competing might be necessary in high-stakes business decisions where specific outcomes are crucial.

However, the *collaborative* style often stands out as particularly effective for resolving conflicts in a way that strengthens relationships. This approach involves working with the other party to find a solution that satisfies both sides, emphasizing problem-solving and partnership rather than winning or losing. This style requires open communication, trust, understanding, and integrating different viewpoints. Focusing on the issue is vital to foster collaboration rather than personalizing the conflict with the individuals involved. This distinction helps maintain objectivity and keeps the discussions productive.

Seeking win-win solutions is central to effective conflict management. This involves identifying the underlying needs of all parties and finding ways to address as many of these needs as possible. It's about expanding the pie rather than dividing it. For example, in a workplace conflict about resource allocation, rather than one department securing all resources at the expense of another, a win-win solution might involve sharing resources or finding alternative resources that satisfy both departments. This approach resolves the immediate conflict and promotes a cooperative work environment.

The *role of empathy* in conflict resolution cannot be overstated. Empathy involves understanding and sharing the feelings of another person from their perspective. Conflict resolution means trying to understand the other person's point of view and emotions, even if you disagree with them. This understanding can significantly change the dynamics of the interaction, shifting it from adversarial to cooperative. It helps break down defenses, ease tensions, and facilitate a dialogue that is more likely to lead to a resolution. Empathy enables you to ask the right questions and engage in a conversation, acknowledging the other person's concerns while expressing your own.

Real-life examples abound where effective conflict resolution techniques have transformed potential relationship breakdowns into opportunities for growth and partnership. Consider the case of a project team in a technology company facing significant delays in a critical project. Tensions were high between the software engineers and the product managers, blaming each side for the setbacks. By applying collaborative conflict resolution techniques, the team held a series of meetings that focused on understanding each group's concerns and challenges rather than placing blame. Through open communication and empathetic listening, they realized that a lack of clear communication about project goals and timelines was the root cause of their issues. Together, they developed a revised plan with clear milestones and regular check-ins to ensure alignment. This approach resolved the conflict and improved the team's overall communication and efficiency, leading to the successful completion of the project ahead of the new schedule.

These examples illustrate the power of effective conflict resolution strategies in turning challenges into opportunities for enhancement and growth in relationships. Understanding and applying these principles enables you to navigate conflicts more effectively, ensuring they lead to positive outcomes rather than relationship damage. As you move through different interactions and face various conflicts, remember the value of collaboration, the necessity of empathy, and the importance of focusing on issues rather than personalities. These tools are invaluable in helping you find common ground, even in the most challenging situations.

5.3 THE POWER OF VULNERABILITY IN BUILDING TRUST

 "Connection requires vulnerability and the courage to be authentic and genuine."

— BRENÉ BROWN

Vulnerability is often misunderstood as a sign of weakness, especially in cultures that prize strength and self-sufficiency. However, in personal growth and relationship building, vulnerability is better understood as a strength—an openness to experiences and honesty with oneself and others that fosters genuine connections. When you allow yourself to be vulnerable, you essentially say, "I trust you enough to show you my true self." This act of trust can encourage others to reciprocate, deepen relationships, and enhance mutual understanding. It's about letting go of the need for control and perfection to embrace being seen for who you are, warts and all.

The benefits of embracing vulnerability are profound. It

allows for deeper connections with others, based not on superficial interactions but on genuine understanding and acceptance. Opening up about your fears, failures, and uncertainties invites others to share their vulnerabilities, leading to more robust, resilient relationships built on trust and authenticity. Moreover, vulnerability can enhance your sense of authenticity, aligning your external behaviors and interactions with your internal feelings and values. This alignment reduces the psychological stress of keeping appearances and promotes greater well-being. Additionally, being open about challenges and imperfections can foster a supportive environment where people feel safe to express themselves and take risks, which is crucial for personal and communal growth.

However, becoming vulnerable comes with risks, requiring careful consideration and skill to navigate safely. One of the first steps in safely cultivating vulnerability is to set clear boundaries. This means knowing how much to share, with whom, and in what contexts. It's vital to assess the safety of the relationship environment before opening up. Trust needs to be earned, so sharing gradually and observing how the other person responds with openness or support can guide you on how deep to go. For example, sharing a personal struggle with a close friend who has shown empathy in the past is different from sharing the same with a new acquaintance or in a professional setting, where the implications could be different.

Leadership often overlooks vulnerability, but it is crucial for building trust and fostering an open and inclusive team culture. When leaders express vulnerability, it humanizes them, bridging the gap between authority figures and team members. It can demystify the image of leaders as infallible and distant, making them more relatable and approachable. This vulnerability can encourage team members to be more open about their challenges and ideas, fostering innovation and collaboration. For instance, a leader admitting to a mistake or discussing their professional development needs can set a powerful example for the team, showing that admitting imperfections and seeking help is okay. This can lead to a more supportive and engaged team dynamic, where members feel valued and empowered to contribute their best work without fear of judgment.

Embracing vulnerability, therefore, can transform personal relationships and professional environments. It requires courage and wisdom to navigate effectively. Still, the rewards—a deeper connection with others, a stronger sense of self, and a more supportive community—are worth the effort. As you continue to explore the power of vulnerability, remember that each step towards openness is a step towards a more authentic and fulfilling life. Whether in personal relationships or professional settings, the courage to be vulnerable is not a liability but a gateway to deeper trust and richer connections.

5.4 NETWORKING MINDFULLY: CREATING MEANINGFUL CONNECTIONS

 "Networking is more about "farming" than it is about "hunting". It's about cultivating relationships."

— DR. IVAN MISNER

Networking often conjures images of crowded rooms; business cards exchanged with fleeting handshakes, and conversations that skim the surface of polite interest. However, when approached with mindfulness, networking transforms into an art form that enriches your professional landscape with genuine relationships and collaborative potential. Mindful networking shifts the focus from exchanging contact information to building meaningful and mutually beneficial connections. This approach to networking emphasizes quality over quantity, depth over breadth, and sincerity over superficiality. It is about engaging with others to foster trust and respect, laying the groundwork for relationships beyond the initial interaction.

Mindful networking is grounded in the *principle of authentic engagement*. This means approaching each interaction with integrity and a genuine interest in the other person. It involves listening intently, responding thoughtfully, and showing genuine curiosity about the person's experiences, challenges, and achievements. For instance, instead of simply asking what someone does, delve deeper by inquiring about what aspects of their work they find most rewarding or challenging. This type of engagement shows that you value the conversation and are interested in understanding more than just their professional role. Expressing your thoughts and contributions can foster an environment where open exchange flourishes. Sharing your experiences and insights in a way that adds value to the conversation can help establish your credibility and demonstrate your willingness to contribute to the relationship.

Applying these principles of mindful networking requires adaptability and awareness of the context in which you operate. Whether you find yourself at a professional conference, a community event, or a casual social gathering, being mindful of the setting and the expected social norms is crucial. Each environment may call for different levels of formality and types of interactions. For example, a conference might provide a more formal backdrop where discussions are likely centered around professional topics and collaborations. In contrast, a social gathering might allow for more personal conversations and informal connections. Navigating these different settings with ease and appropriateness is critical to successful networking.

Building and maintaining a network also involves consistent effort and nurturing. Relationships don't thrive on initial interactions alone; they require ongoing engagement and reciprocity. Regular check-ins, whether through emails, social media, or face-to-face meetings, help keep the relationship dynamic and relevant. These interactions can be about something other than seeking favors or discussing business. Simple gestures like sharing an article you think might interest them or congratulating them on a recent accomplishment show that you value the relationship.

Additionally, providing value to your contacts without immediate expectations of return sets a foundation of generosity and trust. This could mean offering your expertise, connecting them with others in your network, or supporting their events or projects. By consistently providing value and showing genuine interest in their success, you solidify your relationships, making your network a robust community of mutual support and shared growth.

Mindful networking enriches your professional life with contacts and authentic connections that can lead to unexpected opportunities and enriching collaborations. It's about building a network that aligns with your values and meaningfully supports your professional journey. As you engage with others mindfully, remember that each person you meet holds the potential for a beneficial connection and a relationship that could influence and inspire deeper professional and personal growth.

5.5 BALANCING WORK AND LIFE: STRATEGIES FOR HARMONY

"Balance is not something you find, it's something you create."

— JANA KINGSFORD

In today's fast-paced world, achieving a harmonious balance between professional responsibilities and personal life is more than a luxury—it's essential for long-term happiness and health. The concept of work-life balance is often envisioned as a perfect equilibrium where work and personal activities are given equal time. However, viewing it as a flexible relationship is more practical, where the scales tip back and forth based on current life demands. This balance is crucial not only for your well-being but also for maintaining healthy relationships both at home and in the workplace. Work consuming too much time and energy can lead to burnout and stress, which inevitably spill over into personal relationships, causing tension and dissatisfaction.

Practical strategies for managing time and commitments

are pivotal in achieving work-life balance. One foundational strategy is setting clear boundaries. This means defining specific times when you are working and times when you are available for family and personal activities. For instance, you might decide that post-6 PM is reserved strictly for family time, during which work calls or emails are off-limits. This clear distinction helps mentally and physically distance yourself from work, allowing you to be fully present during personal time. Prioritizing health is another crucial strategy. This encompasses physical health—ensuring enough exercise and sleep—and mental health, which might involve activities like meditation or hobbies that help you unwind and de-stress. Ignoring these aspects can lead to a decline in both professional performance and personal satisfaction.

Leveraging technology wisely is also integral to managing work-life balance. In an age where digital connectivity can blur the lines between work and home, it's essential to use technology to support your boundaries rather than infringe on them. For example, productivity apps can streamline work tasks and limit time spent on emails or online meetings. Conversely, technology can also support personal relationships, such as scheduling regular video calls with family if you're working late or away on business. It's about making technology work for you, not against you.

The impact of a well-maintained work-life balance extends deeply into personal and professional relationships. At home, having the time to engage in family activities, attend important events, and provide support when needed builds more substantial, more loving relationships. It shows your family that they are a priority, which can enhance the overall home environment. Employees who feel they have a good balance between their professional and personal lives tend to have higher job satisfaction and are more likely to be productive and committed to their work. This benefits their professional growth and contributes to a positive workplace atmosphere, reducing turnover and fostering team cohesion.

Personal anecdotes further illuminate the benefits of a balanced work-life approach. Consider the story of Sarah, a marketing executive overwhelmed by her job demands, which affected her health and her relationship with her children. By negotiating flexible work hours and committing to leaving the office by 5 PM, she managed to reclaim her evenings for family time. This change elevated her relationships with her children and made her more focused and productive during work hours, leading to a promotion. Then there's the case of David, a software developer who used to work on weekends. After experiencing burnout, he dedicated weekends to his passion for hiking. This restored his energy levels and brought a renewed sense of creativity to his work, leading to innovative solutions that significantly benefited his projects.

These stories underscore the transformative power of maintaining a work-life balance. It's not merely about reducing work hours but about making intentional choices prioritizing personal well-being, relationship-building, and professional success. By adopting strategies that promote this balance, you enhance your quality of life and enrich the lives of those around you, creating a ripple effect of positivity and fulfillment in both personal and professional realms. As you continue to navigate the complexities of juggling various roles and responsibilities, remember that the goal of work-life balance is not to perfect an impossible act but to create a life that feels whole, satisfying, and vibrant.

5.6 EXPRESSING GRATITUDE: STRENGTHENING BONDS

 "Gratitude makes sense of our past, brings peace for today, and creates a vision for tomorrow."

— MELODY BEATTIE

Gratitude is more than a polite thank-you; it's a transformative force that enriches our lives and deepens our relationships. The science behind gratitude reveals numerous psychological and social benefits beyond mere etiquette. When you express gratitude, you're acknowledging the good in your life and amplifying it. Psychologically, gratitude enhances your mood and overall sense of well-being. It shifts your focus from what's lacking to what's abundant. Socially, it strengthens bonds by showing appreciation and acknowledgment of others' impact on our lives, which fosters a deeper connection and mutual respect. This enhanced appreciation can dramatically shift the dynamics of any relationship, making it more nurturing and supportive.

The ways to express gratitude are as varied as the benefits they bring. Simple thank-you notes can capture heartfelt appreciation for specific acts of kindness, reminding both the sender and receiver of the good in their interactions. For something more tangible, consider gestures of kindness like a thoughtful gift or offering help when a friend or colleague is overwhelmed. These acts of kindness don't just convey thanks; they build a foundation of goodwill and reciprocity. Public acknowledgment of a team member's hard work in professional settings can significantly boost their morale and encourage a culture of appreciation. Each method sends a powerful message: I see you, appreciate you and value your contribution to my life.

To truly integrate gratitude into your daily life, consider incorporating practices that encourage a habitual focus on gratitude. *Gratitude journaling* is a potent tool, providing a space to reflect on and record the day's blessings. This practice ends your day positively and trains your mind to seek out and recognize good things, shifting your mental habits towards a more grateful and positive outlook. Alternatively, you could establish a *gratitude ritual*, such as sharing highlights of what each family member is thankful for over dinner. This cultivates your gratitude, strengthens family bonds, and teaches younger members the importance of appreciating life's gifts.

The impact of these practices on relationships is profound. Regular expressions of gratitude can deepen connections significantly, acting as a buffer against the negativity and routine conflicts that sometimes strain relationships. For instance, regularly voicing appreciation for each other's efforts in a marriage can reinforce the partnership's foundation, making the relationship more resilient to stress and discord. Acknowledging a friend's support during tough times can enhance the bond, making it more robust and enduring. In the workplace, a culture of gratitude can reduce competition and mistrust, fostering a collaborative and supportive environment that boosts everyone's performance and satisfaction.

Gratitude, therefore, is not just a reactive expression but a proactive strategy that enhances every aspect of life. Its power lies in its simplicity and sincerity. By making gratitude a regular practice, you enrich your life and bring joy and appreciation to those around you, creating a positive feedback loop of kindness and appreciation. In essence, gratitude is one of the simplest yet most powerful ways to foster happier and healthier personal and professional relationships.

As this chapter concludes, reflect on the transformative power of gratitude and its role in enhancing the quality of your relationships. Consider how implementing regular gratitude practices can change your perspective on life and deepen your connections with those around you. The next chapter will build on these concepts, exploring advanced mindset techniques for personal mastery, ensuring you thrive in your relationships and excel in personal growth and achievement. This personal development journey is continuous, and each step you take builds upon the last, creating a life rich in growth, relationships, and fulfillment.

CHAPTER CHALLENGES

1. Active listening: Practice paraphrasing back to someone at least once a day when that person is talking to you.
2. Vulnerability: Be vulnerable with at least one person weekly to build trust.

3. Define your time: Define specific times for work and family time. Put these times on a calendar or by setting alarms and stick to it.
4. Gratitude: Say or write down five things you are grateful for daily.

CHAPTER 6: ADVANCED MINDSET TECHNIQUES FOR PERSONAL MASTERY

 *"One can have no smaller or greater mastery than mastery of oneself."*

— LEONARDO DA VINCI

I magine standing in front of a mirror, not to scrutinize your appearance, but to engage in a profound conversation with your reflection. This dialogue, known as *self-talk*, is far more than a mere exchange of words. It shapes your reality, influences your behavior, and significantly impacts your journey toward personal mastery. This chapter delves into mastering self-talk, transforming it from a potential adversary into a powerful ally in your quest for a fulfilled and successful life.

6.1 MASTERING SELF-TALK: TECHNIQUES FOR POSITIVITY

 "Your self-talk creates your reality."

— ABHISHEK KUMAR

Understanding the Power of Self-Talk

Self-talk is the internal narrative you hold about yourself; it's the voice that whispers in moments of decision, challenges, and quiet reflection. This ongoing dialogue forms the core of your subconscious beliefs and molds your perception of reality. It can empower or deflate, catalyze growth, or stall progress. Imagine self-talk as a sculptor's hands, where thoughts are the tools that shape the clay of your mind. When these tools are positive, they can chisel out a masterpiece, but when negative, they can mar the beauty of the work in progress.

The dual nature of self-talk means it can function as a barrier and a bridge. Negative self-talk often reinforces fears and doubts, creating an internal narrative focusing on limitations and failures. For instance, thoughts like "I can't handle this" or "I always mess up" diminish your confidence and color your experiences with a shade of predetermined defeat. Conversely, positive self-talk encourages resilience and confidence, painting your challenges as opportunities and failures as lessons. Phrases like "I can learn from this" or "I am capable of more than I realize" are not just words; they are affirmations of your potential and catalysts for your growth.

Techniques to Enhance Positive Self-Talk

Transforming your self-talk requires intentional practice and mindfulness. One effective technique is *affirmations*—positive, empowering statements that counteract and replace negative thoughts. Begin by identifying areas where your self-talk is particularly harsh. For example, if you frequently criticize your professional competence, adopt affirmations like "I am competent and skilled in my work" or "I am growing and improving every day." These affirmations should be recited regularly, ideally at the start of your day or in challenging moments, to embed them deeply into your subconscious.

Self-compassion is another vital technique. It involves treating yourself with the same kindness and understanding that you would offer a good friend. Respond with compassion rather than criticism when you make a mistake or face a setback. Remind yourself that imperfection is a part of being human and that every experience is a valuable step on your path to growth. This shift in perspective can significantly alter your self-talk, infusing it with empathy and encouragement.

Cognitive reframing is also instrumental in enhancing positive self-talk. This technique involves changing your perspective on a situation to view it in a more positive or realistic light. For example, instead of thinking, "This project is going to fail," reframe it to, "This project is challenging, but I have the skills to tackle it." This shifts your focus from fear to confidence and aligns your self-talk with your capabilities and potential.

Monitoring and Adjusting Self-Talk

Becoming aware of your internal dialogue is the first step in mastering it. Practice mindfulness by observing your thoughts without judgment. Notice patterns of negativity or self-doubt, and gently guide your thoughts towards more constructive and positive narratives. Keeping a journal can be particularly helpful in this process. Record instances of negative self-talk and how they made you feel, then write down more positive and empowering ways to frame those thoughts. This helps recognize harmful patterns and facilitates their transformation.

Long-Term Benefits of Positive Self-Talk

The impact of sustained positive self-talk is profound. Over time, it can significantly enhance your mental health, boost your self-esteem, and increase your overall life satisfaction. By consistently engaging in positive self-talk, you reinforce your self-worth and resilience, equipping yourself to face life's challenges with confidence and grace. Moreover, this positivity radiates outward, improving your relationships and interactions with others. As you cultivate a more positive internal dialogue, you'll approach life with greater peace, purpose, and positivity.

By mastering positive self-talk techniques, you unlock the potential to transform your mind and life and influence the world around you. As you continue to practice and refine these techniques, remember that each word you speak to yourself can either be a seed of growth or a weed of discontent. Choose your words wisely and watch as your garden flourishes in the light of positivity.

6.2 VISUALIZATION FOR SUCCESS: SEEING IS ACHIEVING

 "When you visualize, then you materialize."

— DENIS WAITLEY

The power of visualization can often be underestimated in its ability to inspire and drive individuals toward their goals. It's a mental technique that involves the focused use of one's imagination to envision specific behaviors or events occurring in one's life. The clarity, regularity, and emotional engagement with which you visualize these goals can significantly enhance the likelihood of achieving them. Imagine visualization as a rehearsal for success, where the mind and body become attuned to the possibility of achieving intended outcomes, thereby fostering a mindset geared for action and success.

Successful visualization hinges on clarity. This means having a vivid and detailed image of what success looks like for you, whether completing a marathon, excelling in a professional presentation, or achieving a serene state of mind through meditation. The more detailed your vision, the more natural it feels, and the more likely you are to engage in making it a reality. Start by defining clear, precise goals, then imagine yourself achieving these goals, including the environment, your emotions, and even your interactions with others. Engaging all your senses during this process adds depth to your visualization, making it a more powerful tool.

The regular practice of visualization is crucial. Incorporating this technique into your daily routine ensures that it becomes a habit, continuously reinforcing the desired behavior or outcome in your mind. To build consistency, set aside a specific time each day for visualization exercises, perhaps in the morning when your mind is clear or at night as part of your winding-down routine. During this time, focus solely on your goals, using visualization techniques to anchor your intentions for the day or reflect on the steps needed to move closer to your goals.

Various techniques can be employed to enhance the effectiveness of your visualization. *Guided imagery*, for instance, is a powerful method where you guide your imagination to visualize achieving your goals. This can be self-directed or use recorded guides that walk you through the imagery. *Vision boards*, another popular technique, involve physically representing your goals using images, words, or symbols. This is a constant visual reminder of your aspirations and can be particularly motivating. Meditation and visualization allow more profound, more focused engagement with your goals. By calming the mind through meditation, you can direct your mental energy more effectively towards visualizing your success.

The stories of those who have successfully used visualization to achieve significant goals can be powerful inspirations. Consider the case of a young entrepreneur, Emily, who visualized owning her own business. Every day, she would imagine running her successful café, from designing the interior to serving customers. She turned this vision into reality within a year, opening a popular spot in her neighborhood. Then there's Michael, a professional athlete who used visualization techniques to prepare for competitions. He improved his performance by vividly imagining himself executing perfect dives, ultimately winning medals at major championships. These examples underscore the power of visualization not just as a tool for motivation but as a catalyst for real-world success.

You can transform your aspirations into achievable goals by understanding and utilizing the principles of clear, regular, and emotionally engaging visualization and incorporating practices like guided imagery, vision boards, and meditation into your routine. As you continue to practice and refine your visualization techniques, remember that each session is a step closer to the reality you wish to create. With persistence and dedication, seeing can lead to achieving and turning your dreams into tangible successes.

6.3 COGNITIVE RESTRUCTURING: A TOOL FOR DEEP TRANSFORMATION

> *"Thought challenging, also referred to as cognitive restructuring, is a process by which a person challenges the negative patterns of thinking that leads to anxiety."*

—JONNY BELL

Cognitive restructuring is a pivotal technique within cognitive-behavioral therapy, designed to challenge and transform negative thought patterns that can distort reality and hinder personal growth. This method involves:

- Thoroughly examine your thoughts.
- Identifying irrational or unhelpful ones.

- Systematically altering them to reflect a more accurate and balanced perspective.

Cognitive restructuring teaches you to notice when you're telling yourself something that isn't true or overly pessimistic and reshaping those thoughts to promote mental health and personal efficacy.

At the core of cognitive restructuring is the identification of *cognitive distortions*. These are the lenses through which you might view the world in a skewed or biased way. Common distortions include:

- *'All-or-nothing thinking,'* where you see situations in black-and-white categories.
- *'Overgeneralization,'* where you take one instance and generalize it to an overall pattern.
- *'Catastrophizing,'* where you expect the worst-case scenario to occur.

For instance, if you receive criticism on a report and respond with thoughts like "I'm terrible at my job" or "I always mess up," you're likely engaging in overgeneralization and catastrophizing. Recognizing these patterns is the first step in cognitive restructuring and requires a heightened awareness of your internal dialogue.

Once you've identified these distortions, the process of challenging them begins. This step involves questioning the validity of your negative thoughts and assessing whether facts support them or are merely interpretations. Asking yourself pointed questions like "Is there evidence to support this thought?" or "Is there a more positive, realistic way of looking at this situation?" helps break down these distortions and introduces more balanced thoughts. This might mean reframing the thought "I always mess up" to "I made a mistake this time, but I have succeeded in other instances." It's about shifting from a habit of critical self-evaluation to one of balanced self-reflection that acknowledges both strengths and areas for improvement.

Integrating cognitive restructuring into your daily life isn't a one-off task but a continuous practice that enhances mental flexibility and resilience. It requires regular reflection on your thought processes and consciously applying restructuring techniques. Keeping a journal can be particularly effective, providing a space to write down negative thoughts as they arise and actively work on reframing them. Over time, this practice can significantly alter your default mental responses to stressors, leading to profound changes in your emotional well-being and behavior.

Case Studies of Cognitive Transformation

To illustrate the impact of cognitive restructuring, consider the experience of Maya, a project manager who struggled with perfectionism. Her tendency to catastrophize every small error led to constant anxiety and procrastination. Through cognitive restructuring, she learned to identify and challenge these catastrophic thoughts. Instead of thinking, "My presentation has to be perfect, or I'll lose my job," she began to think, "I will do my best on the presentation, and constructive feedback will help me improve." This shift reduced her anxiety and made her more productive and willing to take on new challenges.

Another example is John, a college student who often felt overwhelmed by academic pressures and social comparisons. His common thought was, "Everyone else is smarter and more capable than I am." Through cognitive restructuring, he worked to recognize this as an overgeneralization and began to focus on his progress and achievements. He reframed his thoughts, "I am competent in many areas and can learn from others where I am not." This new mindset helped boost his confidence and foster a healthier, more collaborative attitude towards his peers.

These examples underscore the transformative potential of cognitive restructuring. By learning to identify and modify distorted thoughts, individuals like Maya and John enhance their mental health and unlock new levels of personal achievement and satisfaction. As you continue to apply these principles, remember that each effort to reframe your thoughts is a step towards a more balanced and fulfilling perspective on life.

6.4 OVERCOMING FEAR OF FAILURE: LESSONS IN COURAGE

 "Courage is the power of the mind to overcome fear."

— DR. MARTIN LUTHER KING JR.

Fear of failure is a pervasive force that can paralyze even the most competent individuals, casting a long shadow over personal aspirations and professional ventures. It originates from the deeply ingrained belief that to fail is to disappoint —ourselves, our peers, or the imagined audience we believe judges our every move. This fear is often compounded by societal pressures where success is glorified, and failure is viewed not as a natural part of the learning process but as a humiliating endpoint. The manifestations of this fear can vary widely, from procrastination and avoidance to self-sabotage and decision paralysis. Understanding this fear is the first step towards disarming it, transforming it from a crippling agent into a motivating force that encourages growth and resilience.

To combat the fear of failure, it's crucial to first expose yourself gradually to the situations you fear, a process known as *exposure therapy*. Begin with scenarios where the stakes are low, but the fear is present. For instance, if public speaking terrifies you due to the fear of embarrassing yourself, start by speaking in front of a mirror, then progress to small, supportive groups before stepping onto more daunting stages. Each exposure provides an opportunity to confront your fears, learn from the experience, and realize that failure is often less catastrophic than imagined. This method reduces the fear's power over time, turning daunting tasks into manageable challenges.

Desensitization is another effective technique, especially when combined with incremental goal setting. This approach involves gradually desensitizing yourself to the fear by taking small, calculated steps toward your larger goal. If fear of failure holds you back in your career, set small, achievable goals that lead towards a larger objective. Celebrate each small victory to build confidence and redefine your relationship with failure—from something to be avoided at all costs to a stepping stone to success. This method builds resilience and reshapes your perception of failure as a natural and necessary part of growth.

Building resilience to failure is not about shielding yourself from experiencing failure but embracing it as a valuable teacher. *Reflective practices* such as journaling about your failures and the lessons learned can transform feelings of shame into opportunities for growth. *Mindfulness,* too, plays a vital role in this process. By staying present and non-judgmental towards your experiences, you can observe your reactions to failure without letting them define you. This practice helps cultivate a mindset that values growth and learning over the avoidance of failure, fostering resilience and a more profound sense of personal mastery.

Inspirational stories of individuals who have faced and conquered their fear of failure can serve as powerful motivators. Consider the story of a young entrepreneur, Lisa, who experienced numerous rejections when pitching her startup idea to potential investors. Each rejection fed her fear of failure, threatening to derail her ambitions. However, by applying exposure therapy, she continued to pitch her idea, refining her approach with each experience. Eventually, her persistence paid off when she secured the funding to launch her successful business. Then there's James, a seasoned software developer who feared his new project would fail because it involved skills he hadn't mastered. By setting incremental goals and learning from each setback, James completed the project and gained valuable new skills that advanced his career. These stories highlight the transformative power of confronting and learning from failure, providing practical lessons and hope to those wrestling with similar fears.

By understanding the origins of your fear of failure and actively employing strategies such as exposure therapy, desensitization, and reflective practices, you can see failure not as a threat but as a fundamental element of success. This shift in perspective is crucial for personal growth and resilience, enabling you to pursue your goals with courage and confidence. As you continue to challenge your fear of failure, remember that each step forward, regardless of the outcome, is a testament to your courage and a victory over the limitations you once imposed on yourself.

6.5 THE GROWTH MINDSET: LEARNING FROM EVERY EXPERIENCE

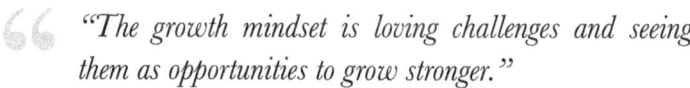

"The growth mindset is loving challenges and seeing them as opportunities to grow stronger."

— DR. CAROL DWECK, PH.D.

The concept of a growth mindset, pioneered by psychologist Carol Dweck, revolutionizes how we understand learning and intelligence. It's rooted in the belief that your abilities and intelligence can be developed through dedication, teaching, and perseverance. This mindset contrasts sharply with a fixed mindset, where abilities are seen as static and unchangeable. Embracing a growth mindset means viewing challenges as growth opportunities rather than insurmountable obstacles. It involves recognizing that failures are not a reflection of your abilities but are chances for learning and self-improvement. This perspective can significantly alter how you approach your personal and professional life, infusing your everyday actions with a sense of possibility and purpose.

Cultivating a growth mindset starts with *changing how you*

view challenges. Instead of avoiding complex tasks for fear of failure, embrace them as opportunities to expand your skills and knowledge. When faced with a setback, instead of conceding defeat, analyze what went wrong and what you can learn from the experience. This approach builds resilience and propels you toward more extraordinary achievements. Persisting in the face of setbacks is another crucial aspect of fostering a growth mindset. It's about maintaining effort and interest over the years despite experiencing hardship and plateaus in progress. This enduring persistence is crucial to mastering anything complex or valuable in life,

Learning from criticism is another essential strategy for developing a growth mindset. Instead of taking feedback personally or defensively, view it as a valuable source of information that can help you improve. Ask questions about the feedback to deepen your understanding, and actively apply this knowledge to future projects or endeavors. This proactive approach to feedback transforms potentially discouraging experiences into helpful lessons that pave the way for personal and professional development.

The principles of a growth mindset can be applied across various aspects of life. In education, for instance, embracing this mindset can transform your approach to learning. It encourages focusing on effort and learning over just grades, fostering more profound engagement with the material and a greater resilience against academic challenges. In your career, a growth mindset can lead to more incredible innovation and adaptability. By viewing challenges as opportunities to enhance your skills, you can take on more ambitious projects and roles, expanding your professional capabilities and impact. In personal relationships, this mindset fosters a healthier, more dynamic interaction where personal growth and support go hand in hand. It encourages you and your loved ones to learn from each other and grow together through life's ups and downs.

The benefits of maintaining a growth mindset extend far beyond individual successes. It promotes continual personal improvement and adaptability, which are crucial in today's ever-changing world. With a growth mindset, you are better equipped to cope with rapid changes and seize new opportunities that come your way. This adaptability can lead to a more fulfilling and successful life, characterized not by fear of failure but by a relentless pursuit of growth. Moreover, a growth mindset fosters a lifelong love of learning, enriching your life experiences and providing you with a robust toolkit to face whatever challenges arise.

By embracing the principles of a growth mindset in every facet of your life, you open yourself to a world of endless possibilities. Whether you're learning a new skill, advancing in your career, or navigating personal relationships, viewing these experiences through the lens of growth and potential can transform your approach to life. It's about seeing every day as an opportunity to expand your horizons and become what you already are and what you might also become.

6.6 BREAKING OUT OF COMFORT ZONES: WHY AND HOW

"The more you seek discomfort, the more you will grow."

— THOMAS OPPONG

Comfort zones are psychological states where one feels safe, at ease, and in control of their environment, leading to regular patterns of behavior that minimize stress and risk. The brain's natural inclination towards energy efficiency solidifies these comfort zones, making the familiar feel particularly comforting. However, the very mechanisms that make comfort zones reassuring also create barriers to growth and innovation. Stepping out of these zones involves overriding the brain's preference for predictability and low risk, which can trigger stress and anxiety, making the process challenging.

Reluctance to leave a comfort zone often stems from fear of the unknown, potential failure, and the discomfort of entering unfamiliar situations. These feelings are rooted in the brain's protective mechanisms that associate unfamiliarity with possible danger, a throwback to more primitive times when unfamiliar territories were fraught with physical risks. Understanding this psychological background helps recognize that the discomfort of stepping out of your comfort zone is a natural reaction, not a sign of personal weakness or incapacity.

The benefits of pushing your boundaries are profound and multifaceted. Embracing new experiences can dramatically boost your self-confidence as you discover you can do more than you thought possible. Each new challenge you overcome is a testament to your capabilities, reinforcing your belief in your ability to handle future challenges. Personal growth is another significant benefit, as new experiences force you to adapt and learn, often leading to the discovery of individual interests and abilities previously untapped. These experiences broaden your understanding of the world, enriching your life's perspectives and enhancing your adaptability, making you better equipped to handle changes and disruptions in life.

Expanding your comfort zone can be achieved through strategies that encourage gradual adaptation to new experiences. Start by setting small, manageable challenges that push your boundaries incrementally. This could be as simple as trying a new food, taking a different route to work, or attending a social event alone. The key is consistency; by regularly challenging yourself, you gradually desensitize yourself to the discomfort associated with new experiences, making more enormous challenges more approachable. Additionally, having a support system is invaluable. Friends, family, or mentors who encourage and support your efforts can make stepping out of your comfort zone less daunting. They can offer encouragement, share their experiences, or join you in new activities, providing a safety net as you explore unfamiliar territories.

Real-life examples of individuals who have successfully expanded their comfort zones can be powerful inspirations. Consider the story of Anna, who feared public speaking but decided to tackle her fear head-on. She overcame her fear by starting with small, informal presentations to friends and eventually progressing to larger audiences. She discovered a passion for communication that led to a career as a motivational speaker. Then there's the case of Ben, a reserved software developer who challenged himself to travel solo to a different country. The trip, filled with interactions with strangers and navigation through unfamiliar cities, significantly boosted his self-confidence and opened up a new hobby in photography.

These stories highlight the transformative potential of stepping out of comfort zones. By embracing the discomfort associated with new experiences, you enhance your self-confidence and personal growth and open yourself to new opportunities and life perspectives. The strategies outlined here provide a roadmap for gradually expanding your comfort zones, supported by real-life examples demonstrating such actions' profound impact.

As we conclude this chapter on breaking out of our comfort zones, we reconnect with the overarching theme of personal mastery. The journey through understanding and pushing your boundaries is integral to developing a more profound sense of self and a fuller engagement with the world. As you move forward, remember that each step outside your comfort zone is a step towards a more dynamic and fulfilling life. In the upcoming chapter, we will explore how these principles apply to individual growth and enhancing professional relationships and career development, continuing our exploration of how a proactive mindset can transform every facet of your life.

CHAPTER CHALLENGES

1. Positive affirmations: Daily say or write down five positive affirmations.
2. Visualization: Visualize your end goals daily for at least 5 minutes.

3. Get out of your comfort zone: Do something uncomfortable for you once a week.
4. Celebrate small victories: Whenever you do something that scares you or is uncomfortable, do something small to celebrate to keep the motivation going.

CHAPTER 7: SUSTAINABILITY IN MINDSET CHANGES

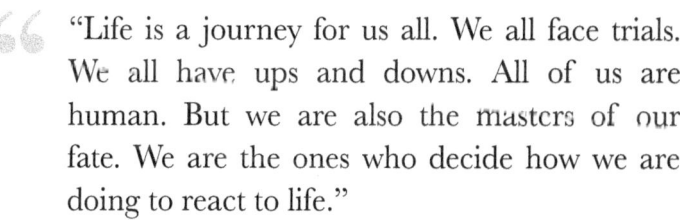

"Life is a journey for us all. We all face trials. We all have ups and downs. All of us are human. But we are also the masters of our fate. We are the ones who decide how we are doing to react to life."

— ELIZABETH SMART

I magine climbing a mountain, reaching breathtaking vistas, only to find valleys as often as peaks. This metaphor encapsulates the journey of maintaining a transformed mindset: it's not a steady climb but a series of ups and downs. Recognizing and embracing the natural ebb and flow of motivation is critical in sustaining the changes you've worked hard to implement. In this chapter, we'll explore strategies that help keep the flame of motivation alive, ensuring that your commitment to growth remains strong, even when faced with inevitable challenges.

7.1 MAINTAINING MOTIVATION: KEEPING THE FLAME ALIVE

 "Always get up and keep moving forward... It may be slow, but it is still progress."

— DIANA MORROW

Understanding Motivation Cycles

Motivation is inherently cyclical, characterized by high energy peaks and lesser activity troughs. This fluctuation is a normal psychological process influenced by numerous factors, including emotional states, environmental cues, and physiological needs. During high periods, you feel unstoppable, as if no challenge is too big. Conversely, during low periods, even small tasks can seem daunting. It is crucial in understanding that these cycles are a natural aspect of human psychology, not an indicator of failure. Embracing this concept helps manage expectations and strategize effectively for a sustained effort toward your goals.

Renewing Commitment Regularly

To keep motivation from waning, renewing your commitment to your goals regularly is essential. This doesn't mean overhauling your objectives every time you face a setback, but rather, revisiting and refining your goals to ensure they remain aligned with your evolving circumstances and insights. For instance, if a career goal set at the beginning of the year becomes unaligned with your emerging interests or industry changes, it's not only sensible but necessary to adjust your trajectory. This flexibility helps maintain relevance and personal connection to your goals, which is crucial for sustained motivation. Setting periodic reviews, quarterly or bi-annually, can formalize this process, ensuring that your goals adapt along with your personal and professional growth.

Intrinsic vs. Extrinsic Motivation

While external rewards like bonuses, praise, and promotions can be effective motivators, they are often less durable than intrinsic motivation, which is driven by an internal desire to achieve for the sake of personal satisfaction. Intrinsic motivation is fueled by finding personal value in the tasks, such as enjoyment, challenge, or alignment with personal values. To cultivate inherent motivation, seek out aspects of your goals that resonate deeply with your interests and values. For example, if you're learning a new language, focusing on the joy of communicating with others in that language can be more motivating than the goal of adding a skill to your resume. This more profound personal engagement makes pursuing goals more fulfilling, motivating, and sustainable.

Role of Community and Social Support

No one is an island, and the path to maintaining a changed mindset is no exception. Engaging with a community or support group with similar goals or challenges can bolster your motivation. Such communities provide emotional support and encouragement, valuable insights, and shared experiences that can enhance your journey. Whether it's a formal setting like a mastermind group or a more informal online community, these groups' collective energy and accountability can be powerful motivators. Sharing your struggles and successes with others who understand can reinvigorate your commitment and provide fresh perspectives on overcoming obstacles.

Interactive Element: Journaling Prompt

Consider maintaining a motivation journal to further reflect on your motivation cycles and enhance your understanding. Regular entries can help you track your motivational highs and lows, providing insights into triggers and effective coping strategies. This practice serves as a personal record of your journey and a tool for reflection and learning.

As we continue to explore the sustainability of mindset changes, remember that maintaining motivation is not about constant peak performance but about understanding and managing the natural rhythms of your energy and enthusiasm. By adopting strategies that acknowledge and adapt to these rhythms, you can sustain the changes you've made, continuing to grow and evolve in your personal and professional life.

7.2 HABIT STACKING: BUILDING NEW BEHAVIORS ON OLD ONES

 "You'll never change your life until you change something you do daily. The secret of your success is found in your daily routine."

—JOHN C. MAXWELL

Imagine trying to build a castle one stone at a time, each representing a new habit you wish to instill. It's a daunting task. Now, consider starting your castle with a sturdy foundation; suddenly, the task seems less formidable. This is the essence of habit stacking, which involves pairing a new habit with an already-established routine. This method leverages the automaticity of your existing habits to anchor new behaviors, making the adoption process smoother and more likely to stick.

Habit stacking works because it builds on your existing patterns of behavior, which are already ingrained in your brain's neural pathways. You create a coupled association in the mind by linking a new, desired behavior to a habitual action. For instance, suppose you want to develop the habit of meditating daily. By stacking this new habit onto your existing morning routine of drinking coffee, you create a linked sequence: coffee, then meditation. Every morning, making coffee naturally triggers the reminder to meditate. This linkage increases the likelihood of the new habit becoming part of your daily ritual, embedding deeper into your lifestyle without the resistance typically encountered when introducing a standalone new behavior.

How to Choose Compatible Habits

Selecting the proper habits to stack is crucial. The key is to identify habits that naturally complement each other and can seamlessly integrate into your daily life. Begin by listing your well-established habits, which you perform daily without much thought, such as brushing your teeth, having lunch, or preparing for bed. Next, identify the new habits you want to develop that logically connect to these routines. The connection should feel natural; for instance, if you intend to practice gratitude, you might stack this habit onto your nightly routine by listing things you're grateful for each night before sleep. The smoother the connection between the old and new habits, the more seamless the integration.

Step-by-Step Guide to Habit Stacking

To effectively integrate habit stacking into your routine, follow these practical steps:

1. **Identify the Trigger**: Choose a consistent portion of your routine to act as a trigger. This could be any well-established habit you perform simultaneously each day.
2. **Choose a Stackable Habit**: Select a new habit that is beneficial and small enough to be completed in just a few minutes at most. The simpler the habit, the easier it is to stack.
3. **Create a Coupled Action**: Link the new habit directly to the trigger, forming a compound action. For example, if your trigger is brewing your morning coffee, the coupled action might be doing a two-minute stretch as you wait for the coffee to brew.
4. **Implement the Stack**: Begin the process of implementation, focusing on consistency. Perform the new, stacked habit every time you engage in the trigger habit without fail.
5. **Review and Adjust**: After a few weeks, evaluate the effectiveness of your habit stack. Is the new habit sticking? Do you need to make the action simpler or adjust the timing? Fine-tuning your approach will help solidify the habit stack.

Examples of Successful Habit Stacking

Consider the story of Lisa, a graphic designer who wanted to improve her hydration but continually needed to remember to drink water throughout her busy day. She created a new routine by stacking the habit of drinking a glass of water with her existing habit of checking her email at the start of her workday. When Lisa checked her emails, she would first drink a full glass of water. This simple stack improved her hydration and increased her productivity by giving her a brief moment to gather her thoughts before diving into her inbox.

Another example is Mark, a teacher who aimed to increase his physical activity. He started doing ten push-ups every time he finished grading a set of papers, a task he did regularly. This habit stack turned idle moments into opportunities for fitness, and over time, Mark increased his strength and overall health significantly.

Habit stacking transforms the challenge of building new habits into an achievable task by anchoring new aspirations to established behaviors. By thoughtfully understanding and applying this powerful strategy, you can enhance your daily routines and make lasting changes that contribute to your personal and professional growth. As you continue to explore and implement habit stacking, remember that the goal is to make your habits work for you, creating a life that feels both productive and balanced.

7.3 THE ROLE OF ACCOUNTABILITY IN SUSTAINING CHANGE

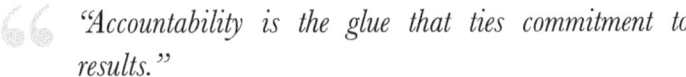

> *"Accountability is the glue that ties commitment to results."*

> — BOB PROCTOR

Accountability, often overlooked, is akin to the silent partner in your journey of personal growth—a force that compels you to uphold commitments and persist through challenges. It functions as both a compass and an anchor, guiding you toward your goals and keeping you steady amidst the fluctuating tides of motivation. Understanding how to harness the power of accountability can transform it from a passive to an active element of success, ensuring that you remain on track even when the initial enthusiasm wanes.

The essence of accountability lies in its ability to make abstract goals tangible. When you articulate your goals to someone else or commit them to a tangible format, they transform from ideas to obligations. This shift is critical in maintaining progress because it externalizes your internal aspirations, making them visible and tangible. For instance, when you share your goal of writing a book with a friend or commit to sending them a chapter each month, the expectation they set can spur you to action. This external pressure, even if friendly and supportive, can be a powerful motivator. It taps into a fundamental human instinct to meet social and personal expectations.

Exploring various methods to establish accountability, one effective strategy is forming *accountability partnerships*. Whether with a friend, a colleague, or a coach, these partnerships provide a structured way to check in on progress, set deadlines, and discuss challenges. The key to a successful accountability partnership is choosing someone genuinely interested in your success and willing to engage in honest, sometimes challenging, conversations about your progress. Regular meetings or check-ins can keep you honest and motivated. Another potent method is making public commitments. You leverage social expectations as a motivator by publicly declaring your goals on social media, a blog, or within a community group. While daunting, the potential for public scrutiny can significantly amp up your commitment to your goals.

In today's digital age, leveraging technology to maintain accountability can enhance your ability to track and sustain progress. Numerous apps and digital tools are designed to monitor habits, set reminders, and track achievements. Tools like *habit trackers* allow you to log daily actions toward your goal, providing visual progress charts that can be incredibly satisfying and motivating. *Often* used in professional contexts, project management tools can be equally helpful in personal goal setting, helping you break down significant goals into manageable tasks and deadlines. The interactive nature of these tools keeps your objectives clear and organized and offers the satisfaction of ticking off completed tasks, reinforcing your commitment through small, consistent wins.

Creating a culture of accountability within your personal and professional life can further embed these practices into your daily routine. Start by setting clear expectations with those around you about your goals and how they can support you. Encourage friends or family members to hold you accountable by asking about your progress and providing honest feedback. In professional settings, foster an environment where accountability is normalized and celebrated. Regular team check-ins, transparent goal-setting sessions, and open discussions about progress and hurdles can achieve this. Such an environment promotes individual accountability and builds a supportive community that values and strives for collective growth.

Incorporating accountability into your life is not about adding pressure but creating a supportive framework that guides and motivates you. It's about integrating your aspirations into your daily existence that working towards them becomes as habitual as the morning coffee or evening wind down. As you continue to weave accountability into the fabric of your growth strategy, remember that each step taken, check-in and update is a building block in the tower of your success, solidifying your path to achieving and surpassing your goals.

7.4 CELEBRATING SMALL WINS: THE IMPORTANCE OF RECOGNITION

 "Your success is a series of small wins."

— JAIME TARDY

The subtle yet profound impact of celebrating small wins cannot be overstated in the quest for sustained personal growth and success. Recognizing even the most minor achievements can significantly enhance your motivation, boost your confidence, and reinforce the behaviors that lead to more significant achievements. This practice hinges on the psychological principle that positive reinforcement strengthens the likelihood of a behavior being repeated. When you acknowledge your successes, no matter how minor, you increase your self-esteem and solidify the habits that contributed to those successes.

Recognizing achievements is a critical feedback mechanism that transforms your perception of progress. Each celebration is a milestone that reminds you of how far you've come and motivates you to continue. For instance, if you're strengthening your public speaking skills, celebrating the moment you complete a presentation without significant anxiety can reinforce your belief in your ability to grow and improve. This recognition shifts your focus from what's left to achieve to what's already been accomplished, providing a psychological boost that keeps discouragement at bay. Additionally, this practice helps to break down larger goals into more manageable, incremental achievements, making the journey seem less daunting and more achievable.

Strategies for Recognizing Achievements

Implementing effective strategies for celebrating wins is crucial in maximizing their motivational potential. One powerful method is maintaining a *success journal*. This tool allows you to document your achievements daily, providing a written record of your progress. Regularly updating this journal is a reflective practice that highlights your accomplishments and lets you visualize your growth over time. This can be particularly uplifting during periods of doubt or when progress seems slow. Another strategy is sharing your milestones with peers, mentors, or friends. This allows for external recognition, which can be incredibly affirming, and strengthens your support network by involving others in your personal development journey.

Incorporating Regular Reviews

Regular review sessions are invaluable for systematically integrating the recognition of achievements into your growth strategy. These monthly and quarterly reviews, or at a custom frequency that suits your goals, provide opportunities to pause and reflect on your accomplishments. Review your success journal during these sessions, revisit goals, and celebrate completed milestones. This offers a moment of recognition and helps you reassess and adjust your goals to align with your current path and aspirations. Regular reviews ensure that recognition is not a sporadic event but a structured part of your growth process, keeping you engaged and motivated throughout your personal development journey.

Balancing Ambition with Appreciation

While ambition drives you to set goals and strive towards them, balancing this drive with an appreciation for current achievements is essential for maintaining a healthy perspective. Constantly focusing only on future goals can lead to dissatisfaction, as you might perpetually chase the next achievement without pausing to appreciate the present. To counteract this, make it a practice to reflect on and savor your current successes before rushing into setting new goals. This balance enhances your well-being by allowing you to enjoy the fruits of your efforts and prevents burnout from relentless striving. Appreciating your current achievements sets a positive, grateful foundation for future ambitions, fostering a cycle of motivation and satisfaction that fuels sustained personal growth.

Incorporating these practices into your daily life ensures that each small step taken is recognized and celebrated, building a ladder of confidence and motivation that propels you toward your larger goals. As you continue to navigate your growth path, remember that every achievement, no matter how small, is a testament to your efforts and a building block for future success. Celebrating these achievements is not just about giving yourself a pat on the back— it's about reinforcing the behaviors and mindsets that will carry you forward in your ongoing development.

7.5 REFLECTION TECHNIQUES FOR CONTINUOUS IMPROVEMENT

"Without reflection, we go blindly on our way, creating more unintended consequences, and failing to achieve anything useful."

— MARGARET J. WHEATLEY

The art of reflection, often underestimated, is a vital tool in your arsenal for personal and professional development. Regular reflection allows you to pause, assess, and recalibrate, ensuring that your actions and goals align with your evolving aspirations and circumstances. This practice goes beyond mere introspection; it involves a structured approach to analyzing your experiences, which can significantly enhance your capacity to learn from them. By regularly evaluating your strengths, weaknesses, and areas for improvement, you establish a proactive approach to personal growth, turning everyday experiences into opportunities for development.

Reflective practices come in various forms, offering unique benefits and suiting different preferences. *Meditation*, for instance, provides a quiet space to clear your mind and focus inwardly, fostering a heightened awareness of your thoughts and feelings. This practice can help you recognize your emotional and mental patterns, which are crucial for personal growth. Writing, particularly *reflective journaling*, is another powerful tool. It allows you to document experiences, thoughts, and feelings, providing a tangible record you can revisit. This helps track your progress and identify specific instances where the learning occurred or improvement is needed. *Structured feedback sessions*, whether with mentors, peers, or through professional coaching, offer a more interactive form of reflection. These sessions can provide external perspectives on your performance, delivering insights that might not be apparent through solitary reflection.

Using these reflective practices effectively can profoundly influence your goal-setting process. For instance, meditation might reveal a recurring stressor that impacts your productivity, prompting you to set stress management goals or seek skills that enhance your resilience. Journaling might highlight a consistent strength in project management, encouraging you to pursue advanced skills or certifications in this area. Feedback sessions might uncover gaps in your professional knowledge or skills, guiding you to adjust your career development goals accordingly. Integrating reflection into your routine ensures that your goals are ambitious and accurately targeted toward areas that promise the most significant growth and fulfillment.

Consider the experiences of individuals who have integrated reflective practices into their personal growth strategies, leading to profound breakthroughs. As a marketing executive, Sarah began practicing daily journaling, which helped her identify a pattern of overcommitment to projects. This insight led her to set more realistic goals, significantly reducing her stress and improving her work-life balance. Another case is John, a software developer, who used feedback from structured peer reviews to pinpoint areas in his collaborative skills that needed improvement. By focusing his professional development on these areas, John enhanced his team interactions and became a leader on significant projects. These examples illustrate how reflective practices can translate into actionable insights that propel personal and professional advancement.

As you continue to navigate the complex landscapes of your personal and professional life, remember that reflection is not just about looking back—it's about learning from the past to optimize the future. Whether through meditation, writing, or feedback, each reflective practice offers a pathway to deeper understanding and more informed action. Engaging regularly in these practices ensures that your development is continuous, responsive, and deeply aligned with your values and goals. This ongoing cycle of action, reflection, and adjustment is the cornerstone of a proactive and fulfilling approach to personal growth, allowing you to meet the challenges of today and shape tomorrow's opportunities.

CHAPTER CHALLENGES

1. Renew your commitment: Renew your goals daily by saying aloud, "I am committed to reaching my goal of _____."

2. Daily journal: Write down any successes you had for the day in a journal.

3. Accountability partner: Find someone you trust who will hold you accountable to reach your goal and for them to check in every week.

4. Feedback: Get weekly feedback on how you can improve from your accountability partner, manager, peer, mentor, or coach.

CHAPTER 8: APPLYING MINDSET PRINCIPLES TO ACHIEVE LIFE GOALS

 "If you really want to do something, you'll find a way. If you don't, you'll find an excuse."

— JIM ROIIN

Imagine standing at the base of a towering mountain, its peak shrouded in mist, symbolizing the lofty goals you aspire to reach. The journey to the summit is not just about the physical ascent but also the mental preparation, planning, and vision guiding each step. This chapter guides you to setting and achieving those goals, not just in climbing mountains but in all areas of life where you aim to see tangible success.

8.1 GOAL SETTING: DEFINING AND PURSUING WHAT MATTERS

 "Setting goals is the first step in turning the invisible into the visible."

— TONY ROBBINS

Clarifying Your Values and Objectives

Before you can effectively set goals, it is imperative to understand what truly matters to you. This clarity comes from deeply exploring your values, those fundamental beliefs that shape your thoughts, actions, and reactions. Identifying these values involves introspection and honesty; it requires you to look beyond societal expectations and focus on what gives you a sense of purpose and fulfillment.

Start by asking yourself what makes you feel most alive, what activities you find inherently rewarding, and what legacy you wish to leave behind. These questions can lead you to uncover integrity, compassion, innovation, or leadership values. Once your values are clear, the next step is aligning your goals with these values. This alignment ensures that your goals are meaningful, motivating, and imbued with a sense of purpose that resonates with your deeper self. For instance, if one of your core values is creativity, setting a goal to take an improvisational theater class or start a creative side project could be incredibly fulfilling.

SMART Goals Framework

With your values in place, the SMART (Specific, Measurable, Achievable, Relevant, Time-bound) goals framework provides a structured approach to setting clear and reachable objectives. Each element of the SMART framework serves a specific purpose:

- **Specific**: Your goal should be specific to make sure your goal is clear.
- **Measurable**: You should be able to track your progress and measure the outcome.
- **Achievable**: While your goal should be challenging, it should also be attainable to avoid setting yourself up for failure.
- **Relevant**: Ensure the goal aligns with your broader life values and objectives.
- **Time-bound**: Set a deadline to create a sense of urgency and prompt action.

This framework helps create well-defined goals and streamlines the path to achieving them, providing clear milestones and checkpoints.

Visualization in Goal Setting

Visualization is a powerful tool in goal setting. It is a mental rehearsal that prepares your mind and body for success. By vividly imagining the achievement of your goals, you engage the same neural pathways as you would when performing the task. This mental practice can increase your confidence, motivation, and commitment to your goals.

To effectively practice visualization, find a quiet space to concentrate without interruptions. Close your eyes and picture yourself achieving your goal in as much detail as possible. Imagine how it feels to succeed, the reactions of those around you, and the steps you took to get there. This process boosts your morale, which clarifies and reinforces the steps needed to achieve your goals.

Regular Goal Review and Adjustment

The dynamic nature of life means that the relevance and feasibility of your goals can change over time. Regular reviews of your goals are crucial to ensure they align with your values and life circumstances. Depending on the nature of your goals, these reviews can be monthly, quarterly, or semi-annual.

During these reviews, assess your progress, identify any barriers you've encountered, and determine whether your goals need to be adjusted or refined. This might mean setting new deadlines, scaling back overly ambitious plans, or shifting your focus to better align with your evolving priorities. Regularly adjusting your goals keeps them relevant and flexible enough to adapt to the continuous changes in your life.

Interactive Element: Visualization Exercise

Visualization Exercise: Envisioning Success

- **Step 1**: Find a quiet and comfortable place to sit or lie down.
- **Step 2**: Close your eyes and take a few deep breaths to relax your body and mind.

- **Step 3**: Vividly imagine one of your key goals. Picture yourself in the process of achieving it. See the setting, the actions you are taking, and the obstacles you are overcoming.
- **Step 4**: Now, imagine having achieved your goal. Focus on the details—where are you, who is with you, what emotions are you feeling?
- **Step 5**: Hold on to the feeling of achievement. Slowly open your eyes, carrying this sense of accomplishment with you.

This exercise can be a powerful motivator, helping you to maintain focus and momentum toward your goals. Regularly engaging in this practice can reinforce your pathway to success, making your aspirations feel more attainable and tangible.

Applying these strategies sets the stage for a fulfilled and successful life guided by clear, well-defined, and achievable goals. This structured approach to goal setting directs your energy and resources efficiently. It aligns deeply with your values, ensuring that the goals you pursue enrich your life and bring you genuine satisfaction.

8.2 OVERCOMING OBSTACLES IN GOAL ACHIEVEMENT

 "Embrace obstacles, as they are the universe's gift to help you overcome whatever holds you back and hinders your success."

— REMEZ SASSON

Anticipating Potential Challenges

As you navigate the path towards your aspirations, it's not a question of "if" but when you encounter obstacles. These challenges are not mere setbacks but pivotal moments that test your resolve and adaptability. The key to overcoming them lies not only in your preparation but also in your mindset. Anticipating potential challenges involves a proactive approach where you visualize possible obstacles and strategize how to handle them. This foresight allows you to develop contingency plans that keep you one step ahead.

For instance, if your goal is to run a marathon, potential obstacles include injuries, lack of motivation, or unforeseen personal commitments. Anticipating these challenges helps you to plan effectively—scheduling regular check-ups with a physiotherapist, setting up a motivational rewards system for each milestone reached, or creating a flexible training schedule that can adapt to unexpected time constraints. By foreseeing these challenges, you transform them from roadblocks into hurdles you are prepared to clear. This proactive approach keeps you moving forward and builds resilience, as unexpected difficulties make you less likely to be thrown off course.

Adaptability and Flexibility

The journey toward achieving your goals is rarely linear. Changes in personal circumstances, unexpected opportunities, or shifts in the external environment can all impact your path to success. Adaptability and flexibility are crucial traits that enable you to navigate this ever-changing landscape. They allow you to modify your strategies and actions effectively to meet new challenges and take advantage of arising opportunities.

Being adaptable in goal achievement means experimenting with different approaches and being open to changing your method when something isn't working. It's about adjusting your sails when the direction of the wind changes. For example, suppose you aim to enhance your professional skills through a specific online course but find that the course doesn't meet your expectations. Flexibility might involve switching to a different program or seeking alternative learning platforms that align better with your learning style and professional needs.

Leveraging Support Networks

No one achieves anything alone, and the role of a strong support network cannot be underestimated in overcoming obstacles to your goals. Your network can include friends, family, colleagues, mentors, or even professional advisors. These individuals can offer emotional support, practical advice, diverse perspectives, and valuable insights to help you navigate challenges.

Effective use of your support network involves being open about your goals and challenges. Regularly communicate your progress and seek feedback. For instance, a mentor might provide guidance based on their experiences, offering solutions you have yet to consider. Similarly, peers facing similar challenges can provide mutual support and share strategies. Remember, leveraging your network isn't a sign of weakness but a strategic approach to broadening your resources and strengthening your resolve.

Mindset of Perseverance

At the core of overcoming challenges is the mindset of perseverance—viewing obstacles not as impassable barriers but as integral parts of the learning and growth process. This mindset shifts your perspective to see each challenge as an opportunity to develop resilience, acquire new knowledge, and refine your strategies. Perseverance is fueled by a commitment to your long-term vision and a belief in your ability to achieve your goals, regardless of the setbacks you encounter.

Cultivating a mindset of perseverance involves regular self-reflection, where you remind yourself of your achievements and the obstacles you've already overcome. Celebrate these victories, no matter how small, as they reinforce your ability to persevere. Additionally, maintain a positive outlook by visualizing the achievement of your goals, focusing on the satisfaction and rewards you will reap. This visual reinforcement keeps you motivated and committed, even when the path gets tough.

By anticipating challenges, remaining adaptable, leveraging your support network, and fostering a mindset of perseverance, you equip yourself with a robust toolkit to tackle any obstacles that come your way. These strategies do not just help you overcome challenges; they transform them into stepping stones towards your ultimate success. As you continue to apply these principles, each obstacle overcome adds a layer of strength and confidence to your journey, enriching your experience and ensuring that when you reach your goals, you are not only prosperous but also wise, resilient, and ready to set new, even more, ambitious goals.

8.3 USING MINDSET STRATEGIES IN CAREER DEVELOPMENT

 "Strategy has no value if your culture and leadership mindset are wrong."

— TONY DOVALE

Growth Mindset in Professional Settings

In career development, cultivating a growth mindset is akin to preparing the soil for a lush and vibrant garden. It's about nourishing the ground with continuous learning and resilience, ensuring each professional challenge is a nutrient rather than a nemesis. By adopting a growth mindset, you embrace the idea that your abilities and intelligence can be developed through effort and persistence. This perspective transforms how you approach your career, shifting from a passive recipient of opportunities to an active seeker of growth.

Imagine facing a complex project at work that stretches beyond your current capabilities. With a fixed mindset, this scenario might trigger fear and avoidance, stunting your professional growth. However, embracing a growth mindset allows you to see this as a valuable opportunity to expand your skill set. It encourages you to engage actively with the challenge, seek learning resources, and view setbacks as lessons rather than failures. This proactive approach enhances your skills and builds resilience as you navigate and overcome obstacles more effectively.

Furthermore, a growth mindset fosters innovation and creativity in the workplace. It drives you to question the status quo and explore new ideas without fearing failure. This can lead to significant breakthroughs and advancements in your field, positioning you as a valuable asset to your team and organization. Cultivating this mindset involves regular self-reflection, openness to feedback, and a commitment to lifelong learning—practices that keep you mentally agile and professionally relevant.

Networking with Intent

Strategic networking is another cornerstone of successful career development. It's not merely about collecting business cards but forging meaningful connections that mutually benefit all parties involved. Effective networking requires intentionality—identifying and engaging with individuals who share your professional interests and values. This targeted approach ensures that the relationships you build are substantive and aligned with your career goals.

When networking, focus on quality over quantity. Seek out professionals who inspire you or from whom you can learn. Approach these interactions with a mindset of offering value, not just extracting benefits. For instance, if you meet a seasoned professional at a conference, instead of merely asking for job leads, engage them in a discussion about industry trends or share your insights on a common topic of interest. This approach makes the interaction more engaging for both parties and increases the likelihood of forming a lasting professional relationship.

Moreover, networking should be seen as a reciprocal process. Maintain your connections by checking in periodically, sharing valuable articles, or offering assistance when possible. This nurtures the relationship, keeping it strong and active, which can be beneficial for future opportunities or collaborations. Remember, a well-maintained network can be a powerful ally in navigating your career path, providing support, advice, and opportunities when needed.

Feedback and Self-Improvement

Feedback is a powerful tool for professional development, yet it's often met with apprehension or defensiveness. To fully benefit from feedback, approach it with a mindset focused on self-improvement rather than self-defense. View each piece of feedback as a gift that provides insights into how you can enhance your skills, improve your performance, and increase your value as a professional.

When receiving feedback, listen actively and ask clarifying questions to ensure you fully understand the points. Reflect on this feedback objectively, separating your emotions from the facts, and identify actionable steps you can take to address any issues or reinforce positive outcomes. For instance, if a supervisor points out that your reports could be more analytical, use this feedback to seek resources that enhance your analytical skills, such as workshops, courses, or mentoring from a colleague skilled in analysis.

Furthermore, actively seek feedback from various sources—supervisors, peers, and subordinates. This 360-degree feedback provides a well-rounded view of your performance and areas for improvement, which is invaluable for your professional growth. Embrace this continuous loop of feedback and improvement as a pathway to excellence in your career.

Career Visioning and Path Planning

Effective career development requires a clear vision of where you want to go and a strategic plan for getting there. Define your career aspirations based on your strengths, interests, and market opportunities. Evaluate what you are passionate about, what you excel at, and where there is a demand for your skills. This triad forms the foundation of a fulfilling and sustainable career path.

Once your vision is clear, develop a detailed career path plan that includes short-term and long-term goals. This plan should outline the steps to achieve each goal, the resources required, and potential obstacles. Regularly review and adjust this plan to adapt to changes in your life circumstances, professional interests, or the job market. This dynamic approach ensures that your career path remains relevant and aligned with your evolving aspirations.

Additionally, incorporate *continuous learning* into your career path plan. The modern job market values versatility and adaptability, so continually updating your skills is crucial. This could involve formal education, professional certifications, or self-directed learning through online courses and workshops. By continuously enhancing your skill set, you ensure that you remain competitive and capable of seizing new opportunities that arise on your career path.

By integrating these mindset strategies into your career development, you equip yourself with the tools necessary for professional success and personal fulfillment. These practices encourage a proactive approach to your career, where growth, resilience, and continuous improvement are at the forefront of your professional journey. As you apply these strategies, remember that your career is not just a series of job titles and roles but a reflection of your journey toward achieving your full potential.

8.4 MINDSET IN RELATIONSHIPS: GROWING TOGETHER

 "Two people in a relationship either grow together or apart over time."

— GREG BEHRENDT

Empathy and Mutual Growth

Empathy stands as a cornerstone in personal relationships, not merely for understanding each other but also for fostering an environment where both partners can grow and flourish. Empathy goes beyond the fundamental acknowledgment of your partner's feelings; it involves profoundly engaging with and experiencing those emotions alongside them. This profound connection can significantly enhance the support you provide each other, particularly in individual challenges or personal growth efforts.

When you practice empathy, you enable a shared journey of development where each partner's growth is viewed as a mutual benefit, not a solitary pursuit. It's about celebrating each other's successes as your own and facing challenges as a unified front. For instance, if one partner decides to embark on a career change, the other's empathetic support can make the transition less daunting and more manage- able, providing a stable emotional base from which to explore new possibilities. This shared growth strengthens the relationship and creates a dynamic where being together propels each of you to greater heights than you might achieve alone.

To cultivate empathy in your relationship, regularly share your feelings and experiences. This can be facilitated through daily check-ins or designated 'sharing' times, which encourage open communication and deepen understanding. Active listening plays a crucial role here; it's about giving your undivided attention, acknowledging feelings without immediately offering solutions and validating your partner's experiences. These practices ensure both partners feel heard and valued, creating a fertile ground for mutual growth and support.

Communication Techniques

Effective communication is the lifeblood of any strong relationship. It's about talking and exchanging ideas, sharing feelings, and building understanding. Good communication involves clarity, respect, and consideration. It ensures that both partners can express their thoughts and feelings openly without fear of judgment or dismissal.

One powerful technique to enhance communication is the use of 'I' statements. This approach focuses on expressing your feelings and experiences rather than making accusatory or general statements, which can lead to defensiveness. For example, saying, "I feel upset when our plans change at the last minute," is more constructive than saying, "You never consider my feelings when you cancel our plans." This method fosters a more empathetic dialogue, focusing on expressing individual feelings and finding common ground.

Another effective communication strategy is the *paraphrasing technique*. This involves repeating back what your partner has said in your own words. This indicates that you are listening and ensures you understand your partner's message correctly. It can clarify misunderstandings before they escalate and help both partners feel assured that their points are getting across.

Conflict as a Catalyst for Relationship Growth

While often viewed negatively, conflict in relationships can be a powerful catalyst for growth and understanding. It provides an opportunity to address underlying issues, deepen mutual understanding, and strengthen relational bonds. The key is managing conflicts constructively rather than destructively.

Approaching conflict with a mindset geared towards resolution and growth involves several strategies. First, it's crucial to stay focused on the issue at hand and avoid bringing up past grievances. Stick to the current situation and discuss ways to resolve it. Next, strive for win-win outcomes where both partners feel their needs have been considered and addressed. This might involve compromise or finding creative solutions that satisfy both parties.

Additionally, taking *timeouts* during heated moments can prevent damaging escalations. If emotions run high, pausing the discussion to cool down can help maintain respect and clarity in communication. Once both partners are calmer, the discussion can resume with a better focus on resolution rather than reaction.

Setting Relationship Goals

Just as individual goals provide direction and motivation, setting shared goals can guide the development of your relationship. These goals can range from financial objectives to lifestyle aspirations or even relational ambitions like improving communication or spending more time together. Setting and working towards these goals fosters a sense of partnership and teamwork and aligns your efforts toward expected outcomes.

Begin by discussing what each of you hopes to achieve individually and as a couple. Find areas where your aspirations overlap and set goals that cater to both partners' wishes. These goals must be specific, measurable, and time-bound, providing clarity and making achieving them more manageable. Regularly review these goals to assess progress and make adjustments, ensuring they remain relevant and motivating.

Setting and striving towards shared goals creates a dynamic of mutual support and collaboration, reinforcing your bond and paving the way for a fulfilling and enduring relationship. This collaborative approach strengthens your connection and ensures you grow together, each step forward in sync with the other's stride.

8.5 FINANCIAL WELL-BEING THROUGH MINDSET ADJUSTMENTS

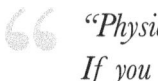 *"Physical and financial health are both very important. If you don't have physical health, you can't do anything. If you don't have financial health, you can't do very much, either."*

— TOM BASSO

Mindset Shifts for Financial Health

When it comes to financial health, the journey begins in the mind. How you think about money profoundly influences how you manage it. Many of us carry limiting beliefs about money that can hinder our financial success. These beliefs may come from our upbringing, experiences, or societal messages and can include notions like "money is the root of all evil" or "you have to work hard to make money." To cultivate a prosperous mindset, it's crucial to challenge and reshape these beliefs. Start by identifying your negative beliefs about money and question their validity. Replace them with empowering beliefs that support your financial goals. For example, shifting from a mindset that sees money as scarce to one that views it as abundant can open up more creativity and opportunity in how you earn and manage your finances.

This mental shift is essential because it sets the foundation for practical financial behaviors. When you believe that you can achieve financial success and that ample resources are available, you are more likely to take actions that reflect this positivity. This could mean investing in your education, seeking higher-paying opportunities, or saving and investing more of your income. A *prosperity mindset* encourages you to look for opportunities to grow your wealth rather than reasons to defend against financial failure. It fosters a proactive approach to money management, where you are constantly looking for ways to optimize your financial health and expand your wealth.

Budgeting as a Mindful Practice

Budgeting often connotes restriction, limiting one's freedom and enjoyment. However, when approached as a mindful practice, budgeting can enhance understanding of one's values and long-term goals. Think of your budget not as a constraint but as a way to direct your financial resources toward what truly matters to you. This alignment between spending and values brings financial balance and personal satisfaction.

Review your current spending and ask whether these expenditures reflect your values and goals. This might mean investing more in health and education rather than fleeting pleasures like dining out or impulse purchases. Each spending decision reflects your priorities, which helps cultivate a sense of control and purpose in managing your money. Furthermore, the future benefits of this alignment should be considered. For example, prioritizing savings and investments prepares you for a more secure and fulfilling future, potentially reducing stress and increasing your options later in life.

Building Financial Discipline

Financial discipline is crucial in turning your financial goals into reality. It involves consistently adhering to financial strategies that build wealth over time. Start by setting up automated savings and investment contributions. Automating these transfers removes the temptation to spend what you might otherwise save or invest, ensuring your savings grow steadily. Additionally, it helps to establish clear financial boundaries. This might involve setting limits on discretionary spending or defining precise rules for when and how you use credit cards.

Regular financial reviews are another essential component of financial discipline. Set a schedule to review your financial status and progress toward your monthly, quarterly, or annual goals. During these reviews, assess your spending, update your budget, and adjust your savings and investment contributions as needed. This helps you stay on track and allows you to respond proactively to any financial changes or challenges that arise.

Wealth Creation Strategies

Creating and managing wealth goes beyond simple savings; it involves a strategic approach to increasing your financial assets. Education plays a pivotal role in this process. Educate yourself about different investment options and their risks and returns. Knowledge about stocks, bonds, real estate, and other investment vehicles empowers you to make informed decisions that maximize your returns and suit your risk tolerance.

Diversification is a crucial strategy in wealth creation. You reduce risk and increase potential returns by spreading your investments across different assets. Consider speaking with a financial advisor to help develop an investment strategy that aligns with your financial goals and risk tolerance. Additionally, staying informed about financial markets and trends can provide valuable insights for making timely investment decisions. Remember, informed decision-making is crucial in wealth management, allowing you to take calculated risks and optimize your financial portfolio for long-term growth.

Integrating these financial strategies into your daily life enhances your immediate financial situation and long-term financial health. Adjusting your financial mindset, practicing mindful budgeting, enforcing financial discipline, and employing strategic wealth creation techniques contribute to a more secure and prosperous financial future.

8.6 CREATING A LEGACY: MINDSET FOR FUTURE GENERATIONS

> *"If you're going to live, leave a legacy. Make a mark on the world that can't be erased."*

> — MAYA ANGELOU

When contemplating the mark we leave on the world, the concept of a legacy often surfaces, enveloping our accomplishments and the values and knowledge we pass on. Defining your legacy involves profoundly reflecting on how you wish to be remembered and the impact you hope to have on others, particularly future generations. It's about understanding that every action and every decision contributes to the narrative you leave behind, shaping how you influence the world after you're gone.

Start this introspective journey by asking yourself key questions: What core values do you stand for? How do those values translate into daily actions? What changes do you hope to inspire in the world? These questions guide you toward a clearer picture of your legacy. For instance, if education and knowledge-sharing are fundamental values, your legacy might involve contributions to educational causes or mentoring young professionals. This alignment of values with actions ensures that the legacy you craft is meaningful to you and makes a positive and lasting impact on others.

Living your values is the most authentic way to build a legacy. It means embodying the principles you cherish most in all aspects of life, ensuring that your behaviors consistently reflect your deepest beliefs. This authenticity attracts others who share or aspire to similar values, multiplying the impact of your actions across communities and generations. Moreover, by living your values openly and consistently, you set a powerful example for others, providing a blueprint for how values can guide successful and fulfilling lives.

Teaching the mindset to the next generations is crucial in extending your legacy beyond your immediate influence. This involves more than imparting knowledge; it's about nurturing a growth-oriented mindset that encourages resilience, curiosity, and lifelong learning. If you are a parent, mentor, or educator, integrate lessons on mindset into your interactions with young people. Demonstrate how to embrace challenges, learn from failures, and celebrate growth. Use stories from your life as examples of how a positive mindset can overcome obstacles and lead to success. This education ensures that your legacy includes achievements, values, and the tools for future generations to build their successful paths.

Sustainability and ethical living are increasingly essential to a legacy in our interconnected and environmentally conscious world. Promoting practices that protect and preserve the environment contributes to a legacy supporting future generations' well-being. This might involve advocating for sustainable practices in your community, supporting environmental conservation projects, or incorporating sustainability into your business practices. Additionally, ethical living—making decisions that consider the welfare of others and the moral implications of your choices—reinforces a legacy of integrity and respect for the community and the planet. These aspects of your legacy highlight a commitment to personal success and the health and prosperity of the wider world.

Embracing the responsibility of legacy creation empowers you to live a life that resonates with meaning and purpose, ensuring that your impact endures through the ages. It's a proactive approach to shaping the future, which values contribution over accolade and collective well-being over individual gain. As you continue to refine and live out your legacy, remember that each choice you make weaves another thread into the fabric of the future, contributing to a tapestry that will inspire and benefit future generations.

8.7 TO LIVE IS TO GIVE: A GIVING MINDSET FOR A FULFILLED, PROSPEROUS, AND SUCCESSFUL LIFE

> *"Give freely and become more wealthy; be stingy and lose everything. The generous will prosper; those who refresh others will themselves be refreshed."*

— PROVERBS 11:24-25 NLT

A giving mindset is a powerful catalyst for success, cultivating an environment of mutual support and collaboration. When individuals adopt a mindset focused on giving, they prioritize the needs and growth of others, creating a network of reciprocity and goodwill. This positive cycle of giving and receiving fosters trust and loyalty, which are essential for long-term success in both personal and professional realms. By consistently offering help, resources, and encouragement, a giving mindset builds a foundation where everyone involved can thrive.

One key benefit of a giving mindset is the *enhancement of relationships*. Strong relationships are the bedrock of success, providing emotional support, diverse perspectives, and opportunities for collaboration. When people feel valued and supported, they are more likely to reciprocate, leading to a network of allies eager to assist each other in reaching their goals. This sense of community boosts morale and increases the likelihood of achieving shared and individual success.

A giving mindset also promotes a *culture of abundance* rather than scarcity. When individuals focus on giving, they operate from the belief that there is enough success, wealth, and happiness to go around. This perspective reduces competition and fear, replacing them with a sense of shared prosperity. In such an environment, people are more willing to share knowledge, resources, and opportunities, which can lead to innovative solutions and accelerated progress for everyone involved.

Furthermore, adopting a giving mindset can enhance one's reputation and credibility. Those known for their generosity and willingness to help are often regarded as trustworthy and reliable. This positive reputation can open new opportunities, partnerships, and collaborations. People are naturally drawn to individuals who exhibit genuine concern for others, making it easier to build influential networks and gain support for various endeavors.

A giving mindset also contributes to personal growth and fulfillment. Helping others and seeing them succeed can be deeply rewarding and motivating. This sense of purpose can drive individuals to push through challenges and strive toward their goals. Additionally, by focusing on others' needs, individuals can develop empathy, patience, and communication skills, all of which are valuable traits for effective leadership and personal development.

Moreover, a giving mindset can lead to a more positive and resilient outlook on life. When individuals are committed to giving, they are more likely to view setbacks as opportunities to learn and grow rather than as insurmountable obstacles. This resilience is crucial for maintaining momentum and achieving long-term success. By focusing on the positive impact they can have on others, individuals with a giving mindset are better equipped to navigate the ups and downs of their journeys.

In summary, a giving mindset is a transformative approach to achieving success. It fosters solid and supportive relationships, cultivates a culture of abundance, enhances reputation, contributes to personal growth, and builds resilience. By prioritizing the needs and development of others, individuals with a giving mindset create a positive ripple effect that benefits not only themselves but also their communities and beyond. Embracing this mindset can lead to a more fulfilling, prosperous, and successful life.

As this chapter closes, reflect on how the principles discussed can guide your actions and decisions, helping you to craft a legacy that truly reflects your values and aspirations. In the next chapter, we will explore how ongoing self-reflection and adaptation can ensure that your personal and professional growth aligns with your evolving goals and the legacy you aim to build. This journey is about constantly growing, learning, giving, and redefining—a dynamic process that makes life a rich, evolving narrative.

CHAPTER CHALLENGES

1. Networking: Join a networking group, whether in person or online; be involved by commenting and asking questions in the group at least once a week.
2. Financial literacy: Take a financial seminar and/or read a book about financial literacy once a month.
3. Leave a legacy: Spend at least 1 hour every week with someone who is a generation younger than

you and pass on your knowledge, wisdom, and experience.

4. Give every day, give whatever you decide to give, whether your time, energy, resources, or money, to someone else.

CONCLUSION

"Graduation is not the conclusion of an achievement but simply the ending of one chapter and the beginning of another chapter." – Thomas S. Monson

As we draw this journey to a close, we must reflect on the transformative path we've embarked upon together. From the foundational understanding of mindset, exploring the crucial elements of growth and fixed mindsets, to the application of these principles across various aspects of life— personal growth, career development, relationships, and financial well-being—we have uncovered the profound impact that our mindset holds over our success and fulfillment.

Remember, transforming your mindset is not a destination but a continuous journey. It requires an ongoing commitment to learning, adapting, and growing. Embrace new experiences and challenges; let them be your teachers. Regular reflection on these experiences will deepen your understanding and solidify your growth. Keep your mind open and agile, ready to absorb and adapt; this is the cornerstone of a genuinely metamorphosis mindset.

Throughout this book, we've discussed vital strategies for sustaining these mindset changes:

- Maintaining motivation
- Stacking habits effectively
- Establishing robust accountability frameworks
- Celebrating each small victory
- Engaging in constant, mindful reflection

These tools are your companions on this lifelong journey, helping to ensure that the changes you make are not fleeting but lasting.

I encourage you to share your journey with others. Engage with communities of like-minded individuals striving to transform their mindsets. Sharing your path can magnify your experiences and provide fresh perspectives that propel you forward. Remember, every story shared is a lesson learned for someone else.

Do not wait for the 'right' moment to start making these changes; the perfect time is now. Choose one principle from this book—perhaps setting a small, achievable goal or practicing daily mindfulness—and begin today. This first step, though small, is a crucial leap towards a broader horizon of possibilities.

Envision your future with a transformed mindset. Imagine a life where challenges are growth opportunities, relationships deepen through genuine connection, and career and personal life are in harmonious balance. Picture yourself empowered by resilience, driven by curiosity, and guided by a deep sense of purpose. This is the potential of a metamorphosis mindset.

Let's remember the holistic nature of this transformation. Aligning mind, body, and spirit is not just an ideal; it's a practical framework for sustained well-being. Nurture your body with the care it deserves, clear your mind through continuous learning and reflection, and connect with your spirit to find deeper meaning and connection in your life.

I invite you to keep this book close, revisiting its pages whenever you face new challenges or set new goals. Let it be a guide that continually offers new insights as you grow and change. Your feedback and stories of transformation are precious, not just to me but to all who walk this path, so please share them.

As we part ways in this format, I leave you with a thought that has long guided me: "Growth is never by mere chance; it is the result of forces working together." - James Cash Penney

Let the force of your transformed mindset be the driving power behind your growth and success.

You are already successful by reading a book and finishing it. Knowledge can be powerful if you use it. Take a light switch, for example. Once you take action to flip the switch on, there is power.

I believe in you! You will be successful!

Keep Transforming

Now that you have everything you need to transform your mind for success, it's time to pass on your newfound knowledge and show other readers where they can find the same help.

Simply by leaving your honest opinion of this book on Amazon, you'll help other people feeling stuck where they can find the information they're looking for and transform their life.

Thank you for sharing this journey with me. May your path be enlightening, enriching, profoundly transformative, and successful. Remember, every step taken in growth is a step closer to the best version of yourself.

-DK Kang

CONCLUSION CHALLENGES

1. Re-read: Re-read this book at least a dozen times. Also, get the audiobook so you can listen to it many times, especially when commuting, working out at the gym, going for a walk, meditating, or cooking.
2. Action challenge: Implement at least one action challenge with every re-read.
3. Rinse and repeat: Read from the start of the book and take action until you mastered your mindset and life.

"Repetition is the mother of learning, the father of action, which makes it the architect of accomplishment." – Zig Ziglar

REFERENCES

Dweck, C. (n.d.). A summary of growth and fixed mindsets. *Farnam Street*. Retrieved from https://fs.blog/carol-dweck-mindset/

Healthline. (n.d.). How to rewire your brain: 6 neuroplasticity exercises. Retrieved from https://www.healthline.com/health/rewiring-your-brain

Lohrenz, C. (n.d.). Overcoming self-doubt: The science of breaking free from limiting beliefs. Retrieved from https://careylohrenz.com/overcoming-self-doubt-the-science-of-breaking-free-from-limiting-beliefs/

Oprah Daily. (n.d.). How to make a vision board that actually works. Retrieved from https://www.oprahdaily.com/life/a29959841/how-to-make-a-vision-board/

Clockify. (n.d.). 26 most effective time management techniques. Retrieved from https://clockify.me/time-management-techniques

Verywell Mind. (n.d.). Procrastination: Why it happens and how to overcome it. Retrieved from https://www.verywellmind.com/the-psychology-of-procrastination-2795944

American Psychological Association. (n.d.). Mindfulness meditation: A research-proven way to reduce stress. Retrieved from https://www.apa.org/topics/mindfulness/meditation

Positive Psychology. (n.d.). CBT techniques: 25 cognitive behavioral therapy techniques and worksheets. Retrieved from https://positivepsychology.com/cbt-cognitive-behavioral-therapy-techniques-worksheets/

CNBC. (2022, December 18). Psychologists: Morning habits to help you be happier, more productive. Retrieved from https://www.cnbc.com/2022/12/18/psychologists-morning-habits-to-help-you-be-happier-more-productive.html

National Center for Biotechnology Information. (n.d.). Mindful eating: The art of presence while you eat. *PubMed Central*. Retrieved from https://www.ncbi.nlm.nih.gov/pmc/articles/PMC5556586/

Harvard Health Publishing. (2014, April 9). Regular exercise changes the brain to improve memory, thinking skills. Retrieved from https://www.health.harvard.edu/blog/regular-exercise-changes-brain-improve-memory-thinking-skills-201404097110

Sleep Foundation. (n.d.). How lack of sleep impacts cognitive performance and focus. Retrieved from https://www.sleepfoundation.org/sleep-deprivation/lack-of-sleep-and-cognitive-impairment

HelpGuide. (n.d.). Improving emotional intelligence (EQ): Expert guide. Retrieved from https://www.helpguide.org/articles/mental-health/emotional-intelligence-eq.htm

National Center for Biotechnology Information. (n.d.). Mindfulness and emotion regulation: Insights from neuroimaging studies. *PubMed Central*. Retrieved from https://www.ncbi.nlm.nih.gov/pmc/articles/PMC5337506/

Greater Good Science Center. (n.d.). Five science-backed strategies to build resilience. Retrieved from https://greatergood.berkeley.edu/article/item/five_science_backed_strategies_to_build_resilience

National Center for Biotechnology Information. (n.d.). Nutrition and fitness: Mental health. *PubMed Central*. Retrieved from https://www.ncbi.nlm.nih.gov/pmc/articles/PMC7353309/

Center for Creative Leadership. (n.d.). Active listening: Using listening skills to coach others. Retrieved from https://www.ccl.org/articles/leading-effectively-articles/coaching-others-use-active-listening-skills/

HelpGuide. (n.d.). Conflict resolution skills. Retrieved from https://www.helpguide.org/articles/relationships-communication/conflict-resolution-skills.htm

Forbes. (2023, March 8). The power of vulnerability in leadership: Experts say authenticity and honesty can move people and achieve results. Retrieved from https://www.forbes.com/sites/luisromero/2023/03/08/the-power-of-vulnerability-in-leadership-experts-say-authenticity-and-honesty-can-move-people-and-achieve-results/

Brogan, K. (n.d.). How to be a mindful networker. Retrieved from https://kristenbrogan.com/how-to-be-a-mindful-networker/

Canfield, J. (n.d.). Visualization techniques to manifest your dreams. Retrieved from https://jackcanfield.com/blog/visualization-techniques-manifest-your-dreams/

Positive Psychology. (n.d.). Cognitive restructuring techniques for reframing thoughts. Retrieved from https://positivepsychology.com/cbt-cognitive-restructuring-cognitive-distortions/

Harvard Business Review. (2018, December). How to overcome your fear of failure. Retrieved from https://hbr.org/2018/12/how-to-overcome-your-fear-of-failure

Strobel Education. (n.d.). Unlocking the power of a growth mindset: How Carol Dweck's research can transform your life. Retrieved from https://strobeleducation.com/blog/power-of-a-growth-mindset-carol-dwecks/

Psychestudy. (n.d.). Motivational cycle. Retrieved from https://www. psychestudy.com/general/motivation-emotion/motivational-cycle

Clear, J. (n.d.). 30 one-sentence stories from people who have built better habits. Retrieved from https://jamesclear.com/one-sentence-habits

Simplilearn. (2024). 25 best productivity tools [2024]. Retrieved from https://www.simplilearn.com/tutorials/productivity-tutorial/best-productivity-tools-to-maximize-your-time

Harvard Business Review. (2021, April). Your burnout is unique. Your recovery will be, too. Retrieved from https://hbr.org/2021/04/your-burnout-is-unique-your-recovery-will-be-too

Oregon State University. (n.d.). SMART goals | Academic success center. Retrieved from https://success.oregonstate.edu/learning/smart-goals

Mind Tools. (n.d.). Visualization - Imagining – and achieving – your goals. Retrieved from https://www.mindtools.com/a5ycdws/visualization

Castrillon, C. (2019, July 9). Why a growth mindset is essential for career success. *Forbes*. Retrieved from https://www.forbes.com/sites/caro linecastrillon/2019/07/09/why-a-growth-mindset-is-essential-for-career-success/

Consumer Financial Protection Bureau. (n.d.). Get money smart: 25 tips to improve your financial well-being. Retrieved from https://www. consumerfinance.gov/about-us/blog/get-money-smart-25-tips-improve-your-financial-well-being/

www.ingramcontent.com/pod-product-compliance
Lightning Source LLC
Chambersburg PA
CBHW051624120626
46551CB00014B/1918